T0278718

AMONG THE
ALMOND TREES

THE ARAB LIST

HUSSEIN BARGHOUTHI

AMONG THE
ALMOND TREES

A Palestinian Memoir

TRANSLATED WITH AN INTRODUCTION BY
IBRAHIM MUHAWI

LONDON NEW YORK CALCUTTA

The Arab List
SERIES EDITOR: **Hosam Aboul-Ela**

Seagull Books, 2022

First published in Arabic as *Sa'akūnu bayn al-Lawz*
by Hussein Barghouthi
© Petra Barghouthi and Áthar Barghouthi, 2022

First published in English translation by Seagull Books, 2022
Introduction and English translation © Ibrahim Muhawi, 2022

ISBN   978 0 8574 2 896 7

British Library Cataloguing-in-Publication Data
A catalogue record for this book is available from the British Library

Typeset by Seagull Books, Calcutta, India
Printed and bound in the USA by Integrated Books International

In memory
of
Alan Dundes

CONTENTS

TRANSLATOR'S INTRODUCTION

Among the Almond Trees is the story of Hussein Barghouthi's struggle with the lymphoma that ended his life in 2004. Dwelling variously on thoughts about death and life and art, it ends with the author imagining himself ascending to the heaven of the Pharaohs upon his death. I refer to the book as a 'memoir', but in his biographical tribute to his father ('Hussein Barghouthi, the Undiscovered Gem of Palestinian Literature'), his son, Áthar, calls it an 'autobiography'. As a masterful work of the imagination that combines prose-poetry and philosophical reflection, it does not fit into the usual frame of fact-based, chronologically oriented autobiographies, though it would be possible to think of it as a spiritual one.

Áthar's tribute to his father contains facts that help provide a context for this work. The most salient of these cover the author's career as a student, first of English literature at Birzeit University, and later of comparative literature—in which he holds a PhD from the University of Washington (1992)—and his work as a teacher of philosophy and cultural studies at Birzeit and al-Quds (Jerusalem) Universities. Before the MA and PhD, Barghouthi studied political science in Hungary for five years. Looking at it simply from the perspective of language, we have here a tri-lingual author whose native language is Arabic but who also has a mastery of English and presumably Hungarian. This work, his last testament, weaves together many strands of thought and experience into a self-portrait of a cosmopolitan writer and thinker who was at home in both Arab and world cultures. I will single out in this context his fascination with mystical religious experience—Sufism holds a special place for him in this work (explored to some extent in the Notes), as does Buddhism, to which he alludes occasionally but which occupies a larger space in his memoir about life in Seattle, *The Blue Light*.

Among the Almond Trees is a highly poetic work of literature, expressed in lyrical prose. The almond tree—in whose shadow most of the action in the book takes place—is its icon. The main preoccupation of the work is time, with a focus on beginnings and endings, expressed in images of light and dark and shadow. This theme is sounded from the very first paragraph. Barghouthi tells us that he had returned to the countryside near Ramallah after an absence of thirty years, and continues: 'I had exiled myself from my beginnings voluntarily and chosen to live as an expatriate. Yet I am one who has perfected 'beginnings' but not 'endings'. The quotation marks are the author's, drawing attention to his approaching (imperfect) end. The work is also, quite naturally, concerned with death. It begins with Barghouthi at Ramallah Hospital, suffering from cancer and suspended between 'the new births on the upper floor and the morgue refrigerator below'. Birth and death, of course, are different ways of speaking about beginnings and endings, and both are manifestations of time. It is the time of the second Palestinian Intifada, and many wounded and dead young people ('martyrs') are arriving at the hospital. He observes that he is not a wounded youth heroically resisting the Israeli occupation army but an ordinary sick person, 'an expression caught between the dictionary of the living and the dead'. We note the intrusion of language as an agent into the discourse of the work very early in the book: the curious expression 'dictionary of the living and the dead' hides a metaphor in which language stands for life, with human beings as words.

The preoccupation with death is demonstrated in the stories the author tells about his family, many of them having to do with (imperfect) endings: the killing of a number of his great-ancestors; the sudden ('preordained') death of one of his great-uncles, and the death of the other from snakebite; the death of his father's friend Yahya while driving a truck in the desert on the way to Kuwait. He relates also that Snuffie, the woman who married both his uncles, had several children from her first marriage all of whom died, while her son from the second marriage died soon after being born. That death and the infant's burial in a cave are described in some detail. She goes through a harrowing scene as a result of disturbing the bones of the ancient dead in order to bury her son in a cave. Even the dead skulls and bones in the cave speak through a spectre that she sees in a vision. The death of Snuffie herself is also mentioned; so is the demise of her Crusader-style house. The spring that the author frequents as a boy with the shepherd Ali is named Qteiliya, the woman who was killed (unjustly); mentioned also is the violent death of Ali himself at the hands of his son, presumably for collaborating with the Israeli Occupation Army.

Yet death does not have the final word; birth does, for the way Barghouthi deals with death is to translate it in terms of new birth, or rebirth: 'Is it not time for my resurrection yet?' he asks. The final paragraph of the book brings together beginnings and endings in one place, and summarizes a spiritual journey in which his death is seen as a new birth into an unusual kind of paradise.

The Mountain is my first beginning, and I pushed it to its utmost reaches: I made it reach Alexander the Macedonian and Al-Mutanabbi and Amon and Ra and the Cape of Good Hope and Lao Tzu and Buddha and Rumi and Baudelaire and Marquez and Mishima, and many such others—many, many others. And in me it has reached as far it could reach; and it, it became itself. I am more conscious of my beginning, so will this Mountain itself, then, recognize in the features of my face that are starting to turn into a strange legend (usṭūra) indeed, will it recognize one of its furthest reaches and one of its endings?' I am one of its "ghreriyas" [badgers], and the time has arrived for it now to see me in the guise of a badger going up, walking up toward the red moon that resembles a goddess contemplating the line of the horizon with eyes closed, saying to me, 'Over there, over there, do you not see? Over there—the ladders of the spirit ascending to the iron sky of the Pharaohs! Go up!'

This paragraph sums up a life from its first beginnings in 'the Mountain,' seemingly before time began (the author's 'first beginning'), to its visionary end in the heaven of the Pharaohs. What Barghouthi calls 'the Mountain' (al-jabal) is a huge hill at some distance from his house, on which sits the Inner Monastery that forms the spiritual focus of this work. It is clear from the destinations to which the text takes the Mountain that Barghouthi is striving for a universal identity appropriate to a poet and philosopher on a spiritual journey, an identity that combines the traditions of East and West. The civilization of ancient Egypt informs the work's visionary poetics, guiding it in the direction of a mythological understanding of identity, time and history. It is primarily a poetics of metamorphosis, as we see in the author's metaphorical equation of himself with the mountain: 'the mountain is my first beginning'. Metamorphosis, or the imaginative transformation of the author's identity, is an ongoing process in the work. In this one paragraph alone, Barghouthi imaginatively undergoes two other metamorphoses—into the legend of the mountain, and into a badger. Death cancels time, and resurrection in the heaven of the Pharaohs cancels death and (calendar) time. As we shall see in more detail, the narrative also plays havoc with linear time.

In becoming 'the legend of the mountain', the author transcends time, like Alexander the Macedonian who conquered the ancient world and built Alexandria and then 'melted, like others, into the folklore of this part of the world, including the heritage of Palestine'. The ending of the author's life on earth will be the beginning of his life as a literary memoir, or as a folktale; or both, and he is the hero of both: 'Yes, yes. I know that my vision of the Inner Monastery and the almond orchards is like a fairy tale.' Once the work of art is accomplished, it becomes timeless, like the leaf that never falls, painted by the ageing painter on the tree in a story he tells about two sisters.[1] The author will live on, if not

---

1 On the leaf that never falls compare the last stanza of Yeats' poem, 'Sailing to Byzantium':

> Once out of nature I shall never take
> My bodily form from any natural thing,
> But such a form as Grecian goldsmiths make
> Of hammered gold and gold enamelling
> To keep a drowsy Emperor awake;
> Or set upon a golden bough to sing
> To lords and ladies of Byzantium
> Of what is past, or passing, or to come.'

—*Collected Poems*, p. 193.

in the heaven of the Pharaohs then on earth in the memory of his readers.[2]

The notion of 'beginnings and endings' is one of the control-ling ideas of the work because it applies to space and time. It is a trope for an understanding of time that is not under the rule of clock or calendar but, rather, is a process of transformation. The plural form negates the notion of a break in time between a known beginning and a determinable ending. This formulation is a kind of shorthand for reincarnation, in which endings set the stage for new beginnings, as we see in his visionary resurrection in the final paragraph. At the top of the Mountain, one can see 'the line of the horizon'. This line is a reference point in space and time, where the sky ends and the earth begins in the transition hours of sunrise and sunset, when the light of day starts to blend into the darkness of night or vice versa with no sharp division between earth and sky. Similarly, this work possesses no sharp divisions, neither of space nor of time, because the writer is poet, philosopher and mystic all at once.

Barghouthi's emphasis on the indeterminate features of the horizon establishes it as the default line of perception in the work. While this line brings together earth and sky in the domain of sense perception, beyond that it stands for the imagination, since it is the site where the author's (and the reader's) imagination unfolds as the memoir is being written (or read) in the present moment. It is also the domain of vision where the mythological

---

2 The theme of immortality through words is expressed directly in the opening lines of Shakespeare's Sonnet 44 ('Not marble nor the gilded monuments / Of princes shall outlive this powerful rhyme'), the couplet of Sonnet 18 ('So long as men can breathe or eyes can see, / So long lives this, and this gives life to thee'), and indirectly in the couplet of Sonnet 116 ('If this be error and upon me proved / I never writ, nor no man ever loved'), among others—*Casebook*, pp. 46, 18, 118.

and the temporal meet in the work, where the moon turns into a reigning goddess and Barghouthi sees himself being born from a shining star. As we see from the last paragraph of the book, the author imagines reaching a spiritual or visionary state in which he becomes one with the Mountain. The separation between subject and object is overcome in the poetry of the writing, and in that state of oneness the author ascends from the line of the horizon, up along the 'iron ladder', to the first heaven of the Pharaohs. In the form of this memoir, the author will become the legend of the Mountain; and, as the memoir ends in his anticipation of death, his ending will also be the imagined end of the Mountain: 'so will this Mountain itself, then, recognize in the features of my face that are starting to turn into a strange legend (usṭūra) indeed, will it recognize one of its furthest reaches and one of its endings?' History comes to an end with the death of the individual. What remains are stories.

Barghouthi's reflections on time grapple with the meaning of time itself, from the notion of calendar time, to historical processes, to resurrection and then reincarnation, and to the possibility of a timeless existence in myth and literature. These reflections include thoughts on the negation of time, expressed in his thoughts about 'the lost time':

> One day, the ancient Pharaohs decided to change their lunar year from 365 days to 360. In thus changing the calendar, the Pharaohs cancelled time altogether, or at least created a hiatus in which it ceased to exist. To a certain extent, this means that anyone born during these five days would also be born 'in lost time', and that in turn means birth 'in a more ancient and more authentic time', one that memory 'has forgotten or pretends to forget'.

Reincarnation, in which (for those who believe) the eternal soul is translated back into history by means of its perpetual return, and 'lost time', which is time that exists outside memory, are both mythological perspectives on the origin and meaning of time.

Resurrection as a motif occurs on a number of occasions, of which I will single out his remarks on his infant son tracing the movement of an Israeli military helicopter with his head 'under the faint light of the candle as if he were following his destiny, or as if he were a sunflower shadowing (literally, 'in pursuit of') a day of resurrection'. In the sunflower that shadows a day of resurrection we have the union of the earthly and the heavenly. The shift of perspective to a sunflower that sees sunset and sunrise as its day of resurrection borders on the sublime. (The first stanza of William Blake's poem, 'Ah! Sunflower' comes to mind here).[3] The sun is the Egyptian god Ra (mentioned in the quoted final paragraph), who travels on a boat that carries him through the underworld overnight and brings him back, to be reborn at dawn. In the symbol of a sunflower chasing its destiny the poet manages to encapsulate the myth of Ra in a single image. Mythology and poetry are indissolubly linked in the power of the image.

As for reincarnation, it is a reaffirmation of the experience of the unity of all being that we encounter throughout the work: 'The words forgotten since my previous life awakened in the eternal cycle of reincarnation, thanks to which everything returns, but does not return exactly the same.' Two states stand out in symbolizing this return: return to childhood ('And I will go back to being a child again') and a more ancient return as a plant form: 'Is it not time for my resurrection yet? I will ripen shortly with the almonds, pomegranates and roses.' In another place he sees him-

---

3 'Ah, sunflower, weary of time, / Who countest the steps of the sun, / Seeking after the sweet golden clime / Where the traveller's journey is done.' —*The Complete Poems*, p. 221.

self and his wife reborn as olive trees: 'Áthar will grow up here, near the shadows of my memory, with my wife and myself as the two olive trees.' The shadows of the olive trees that are the plant forms of him and his wife are the same shadows of the trees in the orchard that he had walked in when alive. In any case, a human being is not necessarily composed of solid substance: 'And I felt that a human being is a light shadow, moonlit and fluctuating between two powers: the power of skeletons scattered about in a stone basin from Roman times, and a power that raises him to higher ground, like the cypress and pine trees and the gazelle and the wild thyme.' The first power is that of time that turns human beings into brittle bones, and the second is that of rebirth that raises them to a state of oneness with all beings. And, of course, his own burial in the orchard will transform his body into the landscape. The notion of reincarnation thus enables us to see Barghouthi still hovering over the landscape in his virtual body, just as he had filled it with his presence when walking in the moonlit shadows, himself a shadow, as he says, in the orchards at night. He may be dead and buried, but he has not left his beloved landscape—the silent hero of this memoir.

Much of the action in the book takes place at night, because night brings together all the elements of nature and imagery that fit the theme of death. The light of the moon creates in the shadows of the trees a chiaroscuro space between light and dark, domestic and wild, where the author meets creatures like the badger, the wild boar and the foxes; and where strange events, like the dance of the gazelles, take place. Night is also when his aunt indulged in her 'magical' practices, when he listened to his mother narrate folktales, and when his uncle recited episodes from the oral epic *Al-Zir Salem*. The most famous work in Arabic literature is the collection of oral / written folktales that we know as *The Thousand and One Nights*—a reference to the number of nights over which Shahrazad stretches the reach of her tales in order to save herself from execution by her tyrant of a husband. In the Arabic narrative tradition, tales are told at night, and narration is equated with life. It is clear that Barghouthi consciously fits his memoir into that tradition, for, like Shahrazad, he weaves in and out of stories and stories within stories, scrambling time altogether. Like the *Thousand and One Nights*, it is a tale that gives symbolic life to one who, also like Shahrazad, is under judgement of death, one who turns the act of writing under these circumstance into a heroic act of narration: 'Perhaps with these tales I could breathe the air of other places and other times in order to sense another moonlit space inside my being and return to whatever inner monastery there was in my spirit that would grant me the strength of beginnings so that I could face the cruelty of endings. For imagination is power.'

Toward the end of the book, the author, in recollecting his family's history at the Inner Monastery, assumes the identity of his great-uncle, and has another vision: 'I will sit on the roof of our house and play [the rabab], exactly like Qaddura, and look over deep moonlit valleys and cultivated orchards, and with all of this I will have completed another cycle in the eternal cycle of reincarnation and another folktale of the mountain. Another cycle, and another fairy tale!' Folktales run in cycles and share plots across cultures such that each folktale has been given a Type number in the Aarne-Thompson-Uther Index. Due to his understanding of the continuity of life in reincarnation, the author sees history itself as a cycle, or cycles, of folktales. Not only is there no beginning and no ending, but there is no individual history altogether. There is only the collective identity of the word, spoken and written.

Rebirth of the soul was one of the beliefs of the ancient Egyptians about the afterlife, and Barghouthi may have encountered it there, but I think it is more likely his exposure came from Eastern religions (that quoted paragraph tells us he made the Mountain reach Buddha) when he was living in Seattle. Reincarnation, after all, is fundamental to the eschatology of both Buddhism and Hinduism. Closer to home, the Druze also hold with reincarnation, and it is there that Barghouthi turns to understand the significance of the fact that the first word his son spoke was *aeroplane*. The birth of his son was an event that had such a profound impact on his life, particularly after he had been diagnosed with cancer, that it gave him an intimation of immortality in historical time: 'I don't understand the meaning of these paradoxes that interlock my life with his. As if he were me; or as if I were him.'

A Druze elder living in the Israeli occupied Golan Heights explains the meaning of reincarnation this way: 'When a child speaks the first word, we, the Druze, say, '"He has spoken,' and thus has entered the cycle of reincarnation." An older soul settles into the new-born, and speaks its first words through him—perhaps the beginning of its own past, or the beginning of its future.' The last phrase presents us with another paradox of time: we can understand what the beginning of the future means, but in order to comprehend the beginning of the past we have to think of time going backwards as well as forward, as it in fact does in the narrative part of this memoir, taking us back and forth in time, engaging our imagination and replicating the world view of the author in the structure of the work. The Druze elder in effect says that history begins with the child's entry into language—an idea that would certainly appeal to a poet who sees human beings as expressions of language, itself the instrument of transformation.

Biographical time, on the other hand, is measured by events, including his marriage, the birth of his son, a trip to the Red Sea, the marriage of his father to his mother, the building of his house, his visits to the Inner Monastery accompanied by his wife and his son, and the numerous visits he makes to hospitals and cancer clinics. Subjective time consists of stories from his childhood, especially when listening to the folktales of his mother, and the hours he spent as a child in the company of Ali, the Shepherd. A great part of the narrative, however, takes place in visionary time, and is devoted to recollections of his walks on the Mountain with his son to 'ring the bell of the world', and to his encounters with various wild animals in the moonlit orchards. Perhaps due to the acute awareness of approaching death, there is a heightened experience of the moment, which the narrative follows outwardly in the external observation of the landscape and its shadows, and inwardly in subjective contemplation. The reader accompanies him on this last journey of awareness in the present tense of the verb—the dominant tense in the book: '. . . over there, over there, do you not see? Over there—the ladders of the spirit ascending to the iron sky of the Pharaohs! Go up!' There is a convergence of the word and the action here; in the present moment the word is the action.

Language is a living presence as a thing-in-itself in the memoir, aside of course from being the medium of communication. A number of topics suggest themselves here, as in his reference to the strange behaviour of the cat that usually accompanied him on his walks in the moonlit orchards: 'I believed it had something to say to me with movement, rather than utterance, and with meowing, rather than in the prevalent languages.' This is a strange utterance itself, its implication being that cats can speak different languages. Perhaps we can understand it from the perspective of reincarnation: we recall the author's words about returning, but not exactly 'in the same form'. There is also a reference to the strange language of childhood when Áthar constructs a story about the moon being afraid of iron: 'An enchanting language for a more enchanting fable!'

The most important manifestation of language as a thing in itself is Barghouthi's extended reflection on names and naming, which is really about the truth of language (or *in* language). The question of names and naming (and it is a question) engages the philosophical side of the writer; for names name things, yet the thing passes and the name remains. Thus names join the historical with the timeless, as we will see when we look at the author's fascination with Alexander. Reflection on the name branches out into the personal, the historical, and the political. At the personal level, his name, Barghouthi, is an attribute of 'the flea' ('that which is flea-like'), and when his wife asks him why they named his family after the fleas, he ironically suggests they that, rather, they were named 'after the lions'. Her original name, Eiman ('faith') is a popular one in the Arab world.

The poetic impulse in this work (as perhaps in all poetry) is to make the abstract concrete; and this, I believe, was the source of his notion of the 'city of the name'. The idea here is that people who have the same name, by virtue of that fact, share a greater degree of affinity than those who happen to have the same city as their birthplace. The city of the name is thus the city that belongs to the name, and its existence depends on the shared feature of language among its inhabitants. In renaming his wife Petra, Barghouthi gives her a second birth in a name that is connected with a beautiful city carved in pink rock that he himself identifies with. The city is also connected with the history of a Nabatean Arab civilization that flourished between 150 BCE, and 150 CE. Barghouthi was baffled about what to name his son, until the name Áthar was revealed to him in a dream. (The linguistic complexities of this name are discussed in the Notes to the memoir itself.)

This fantasy of the city of the name may at first seem to be a mere poet's fancy, yet especially applied to the people of Rusaifa in Jordan, it serves as an important reminder of the Palestinian Nakba that turned them, as well as three quarter of a million others, into refugees in Arab countries. They, like the refugees from 1948 who settled within the country in camps in the Jordan Valley and were driven out again during the 1967 War, share their names with cities to which they are denied the right to return. Petra herself is a 1948 refugee. There is perhaps no better description of the Nakba than Barghouthi's estimation that living outside Palestine as a refugee is equivalent to living in hell: 'And what kind of hell is Rusaifa? A city of Khamsin dust, and a desert noon that feels like a "reality fried to 45 degrees Centigrade".'

In Petra, Barghouthi sees a monument of an Arab civilization with continuities to the monumental civilization of Egypt: 'the sculptors of this city carved their will into the rock in worship of permanence and beauty, like their brothers, the builders of the Pyramids who discovered the art of embalming mummies'. In reflecting on the city of Petra, the author's focus is not only on the monumentality of the place but also on of one of his other themes, cultural and linguistic continuity: 'From this place came the Nabatean alphabet, from which descended the Arabic alphabet that I am now using to write. They carved a city in rock, and another in the alphabet.' His sense of Arab cultural continuity is violated when he is made to pay the same (very expensive) entrance fee to the monument that a foreign tourist pays: 'In vain did I try to convince the employee selling tickets that I was not a "foreigner" to my heritage, nor to his.' Barghouthi is treated as a foreigner in Arab land due to artificial divisions created by colonizing foreign powers: 'Even the name of your son Áthar was thought to be Arthur, a foreign name, a name coming from those who colonized you; no one even considered that it comes from the Arabic language. What a loss that you should lose your identity to such an extent!'

Among the Almond Trees is suffused with light, whether it is that of the moon, the sun or the stars; the faint red light of the Ramallah Hospital corridor, the depressing white lights of the cancer clinic; the halogen lights of the Israeli Settlement; the light supplied by the power company; the flickering light of a candle, a charcoal fire, an Israeli helicopter, or a firefly; the pale yellow light in which he sees the weasel; the blue of the whale and the blue of the imagined American film; the haze of a Rusaifa sunset, or the gilded yellow of the 'villa' he rents near Amman, in Jordan; the suffocating light of the Khamsin wind; the silver of the foam on the shore of the Red Sea, to name only a few. Colours—the hopeful colours of nature, the chiaroscuro of the line of the horizon, the contemplative colour of moonlight and the stars, the colours associated with sickness—are used as guides to the author's emotions. Wherever we look in this work we find the word *light*, which I see as the visual equivalent of birth: 'My beginnings are not from a point, but from a star that shines.' To see fresh birth everywhere—in the birth of his son, in nature in spring, in his own thought, in himself as a form of nature being born, in his own birth from light—is a visionary or mystical state of oneness with the world that the author reaches for through the poetry of his prose.

Earlier, I noted that, after his burial among the almonds, the author and the landscape will become one, but landscape is also geography. In reviewing the various 'places' that Barghouthi made the Mountain reach, I referred to his 'cosmopolitan' identity, by which I meant a cultural Levantine identity that includes Egypt.

The Levant constitutes a cultural unit that provides Barghouthi's historical and geographic sense of identity, centred on the figure of Alexander. In Alexander's wake came the flowering of Greek civilization in the Levant that we call Hellenism. I think what fascinates Barghouthi about Alexander is that he brought European civilization to a Semitic region, and then turned 'native.' Alexander was adopted by the region that started to weave legends about his birth and his exploits immediately after his death, claiming him as her own: 'Alexander the Macedonian conquered the ancient world, and built Alexandria. Then he melted, like others, into the folklore of this part of the world, including the heritage of Palestine.' Alexandria was to become the ultimate cosmopolitan city and the intellectual centre of what we now call the Middle East for many centuries after its founder's death. Like the author, the historical Alexander metamorphosed into his legends.

I think Barghouthi saw himself as a cultural Alexander in reverse—a Middle Easterner who spent thirty years in Europe and the United States, adding to his Arab heritage the cultural dimensions of Western education and then returning to his native land as a cosmopolitan inheritor of all these traditions. Not mentioned directly but by implication is the identification of Alexander with the Palestinian Christ through immaculate conception from the Egyptian god Amon (also mentioned in that final paragraph) by means of the magical power of the soothsayer, Nectanebus. This myth of the magical birth of Alexander is perhaps the foundation of Barghouthi's preoccupation with the notion of birth: 'In birth there is an enigma.' Though it may be far-fetched to say so, there is more than a remote hint that Barghouthi thought of himself as one of Alexander's reincarnations: 'I have roots in Egypt, and in the Two-Horned Alexander.' Elsewhere he says, quoting Nietzsche, that it is 'banal to consider a person as the son of his father and mother. I can be the son of Alexander the Great, as Alexander himself was the son of Amon and not of Philip.' The transformation of the historical Alexander into legends is part of the transformation of historical events into narratives, and personal life into memoirs.

A second Egyptian contribution to the work is spiritual, which I think of as encompassing his poetic imagination as well as the eschatological concern with resurrection. Regarding the imagination, the preoccupation of the writing with soothsayers and Egyptian magic may seem strange at first, until we realize that prophecy and poetry have been associated from ancient times. Something his son says seems to him prophetic, and he mentions (as noted earlier) that he wants to return as a child-prophet. The modern English adjective *vatic*, meaning 'oracular' or 'prophetic,' is derived from the Latin word for poet, *vates*. One of the greatest Arab poets mentioned in the text (and again in the final paragraph) is Al-Mutanabbī—'the one who claims prophecy'. Barghouthi confirms that he sees himself in that capacity when he identifies himself with Tiresias: 'I felt I was Tiresias, the oracle of Delphi in the Fourth Century BCE. I was not of this age, and I began to recite lines from T. S. Eliot's *The Wasteland*: 'I, Tiresias, saw all of this'.[4] The end of this process is the author assuming the guise of a soothsayer who roams the wild spaces: 'I thought as I stared into the mirror that all I needed was a long yellow robe, suitable for a soothsayer or a child prophet, an ancient sandal made of leather, and immense toenails suitable even for tramping in swamps.' In approaching death, the author turns to the Near Eastern civilization that devoted so much of its energy to the arts of defeating death, creating the monuments that still move us to awe and wonder.

---

4 'I, Tiresias, old man with wrinkled dugs/ Perceived the scene, and foretold the rest'.—*The Wasteland*, III (The Fire Sermon).

'Tramping in swamps' and 'immense toe nails' are meant to give the impression of wildness, and the word *wild*, in fact, dominates this work. It arises from Barghouthi's conception of himself as a wild person—an outsider who does not fit into the culture. His fascination with the gypsies, together with his self-identification as one in his song '*Anā Nawarī*' ('I'm a gypsy') is part of this self-image. Barghouthi even takes on the aspect of wildness in his appearance, where the line of separation between him and nature seems to dissolve: 'Even my [long] hair felt as though it grew out of my skin like chrysanthemums and ears of wheat, as if I were a field or an archaeological mound.' This feeling of wildness and of being an outsider predates the lymphoma; it is therefore possible to see that the uncontrollable growth taking place in his body is further confirmation of that already-existing wildness: 'Because of the inflammation in my lungs and windpipe, when I breathe I produce sounds stranger than this singing of the Mountain, a rattle that resembles a wounded mythical animal . . . The sounds intermingle, as if there were a forest in my throat.'

Wildness is also manifest in the weather, with the arrival of the Khamsin wind that he describes in minute detail. Even nature seems disturbed during the Khamsin; the writing strikes an apocalyptic note in its description of the strange effects produced by the light emanating from the minaret of the village mosque when the sun has been blanked out by dust. The end of time seems to have arrived, except for the bird that struggles against the wind on the pomegranate branches and finally flies away sideways to protect itself from a direct onslaught. That bird is a symbol for the author, struggling against the force of nature that is cancer. The sideways manner in which the bird flies away ('the swerve') leads to a reflection on the nature of art and poetry, and this may in fact be an apt description for the memoir—a sideways deflection of the Khamsin wind blowing through his body.

The historical dimension of time is anchored in what Barghouthi calls 'the memory of place', dhākirat al-makān. The meaning of this complex phrase turns back upon itself: it has a transitive meaning—the memory that people have of a place—as well as an intransitive one—the collective memory that a place has of the people who have lived in it. All Palestinian memoirs are tied firmly to the memory of place. Jabra Ibrahim Jabra is rooted in Bethlehem and the landscape surrounding it. Though she lives in London, Ghada Karmi's Memoir *In Search of Fatima* returns to Jerusalem, describing with great care the house where she was born and the events that led her family to leave it. Practically all of Mahmoud Darwish's writing holds close the memory of place (Birwe, the village in which he was born, Haifa, the Galilee, and the land of Palestine as a whole). 'What gives the land all this wildness except desertion?' Darwish asks in *Journal of an Ordinary Grief.*[5] In his volume of poetry *Why Did You Leave the Horse Alone?* the boy asks, 'Why did you leave the horse alone?' and his father answers, 'To keep the house company, my son, / Houses die when their inhabitants are gone'.[6] Barghouthi uses the notion of the 'memory of place' in order to contrast Palestinian memory with the memory of the Israeli settlers living inside 'an armed vision', surrounded by a barbed wire fence and bright halogen lights that destroy the beautiful shadows of the landscape in the moonlight.

This idea of the 'memory of place' is Barghouthi's profound summation of Palestinian cultural and folk history. This memory is ancient, forming part of the identity of Palestinians as a people long before the rise of the national liberation movement. Christians take it back to the time of Christ, Muslims to the rise of Islam

---

5 *Journal of an Ordinary Grief*, p. 16.
6 *Why Did You Leave the Horse Alone?* p. 30.

in the seventh century CE, when Jerusalem became the site of the Prophet's mystical night journey, and historians take it back even further, to the Canaanites. To preserve their memory and cultural identity, Palestinians organized their refugee camps in such a way as to resemble the villages from which they were driven out. When a refugee-camp child is asked where he or she is from, they will give the name of the village or town in Palestine where their grandparents were born, as Barghouthi says of the inhabitants of Rusaifa. The proliferation in the United States and elsewhere of social clubs that carry the name of a Palestinian town or village is proof of this fact. Palestinian historians have written books documenting the villages and towns destroyed by Israel after its establishment in 1948. They have also created a huge archive of that collective memory on the Internet.[7]

---

7 For village histories, see Rochelle Davis, *Palestine Village Histories: Geographies of the Displaced* (2011): 'More than 120 *village memorial books* about the more than 400 villages that were depopulated and largely destroyed in the 1948 Arab-Israeli war have been published. Compiled as documentary histories and based on the accounts of those who remember their villages, they are presented as dossiers of evidence that these villages existed and were more than just a 'place on the map' (p. *xvii*).

For the destroyed villages, see Walid Khalidi, *Before Their Diaspora: A Photographic History of the Palestinians, 1876–1948* (1984). For a general history of the Nakba, see Nur Masalha, *The Palestine Nakba: Decolonising History, Narrating the Subaltern, Reclaiming Memory* (2012). For the ethnic cleansing of Palestine, see Ilan Pappe, *The Ethnic Cleansing of Palestine* (2006).

On Palestinian children remembering where their grandparents are from, compare Mahmoud Darwish:

During the June War [of 1967] many Israeli soldiers were surprised that Arabs have a memory, and remember a homeland that was lost. What surprised them most was that most of the children born after the loss of the country were still attached to it. An Israeli soldier related that when he went into one of

A happy surprise for me as a literary folklorist was the degree to which Palestinian folklore was woven into the fabric of the narrative: 'Stories are the windows of the spirit and the imagination'. The title of the second chapter, 'The Land of Tales', which places geography and folk stories under the same roof (so to speak), provides the rationale for the prevalence of folklore in this work, where we can discern three interlocking streams serving complementary purposes: folk customs and beliefs, stories that have their basis in history, and tales that belongs to the domain of the imagination. The folk customs-and-beliefs stream includes stories about flying snakes, stories of origin (the nay, and the name of the Qteiliya spring), the extended description of customs like Thursday of the Dead (no longer current in the country), the one-stringed folk instrument known as the rabab, the magical practices of his aunt, the stories about the death of her son and her cave, and the importance of the marriage dowry. The author claims his Palestinian identity through emphasis on the folklore of his people as it manifests itself in his experience.

The folklore that is rooted in the imagination includes the folktales and legends Barthoughi either mentions or recounts. Al-Khader is unquestionably the most important Palestinian saint for both Muslims and Christians. His icon—found in every Greek Orthodox and Greek Catholic church in the country—is a knight (St George) on a horse with a harpoon in his right hand, arm raised to thrust it into the mouth of a dragon gaping up at him.

---

the refugee camps he discovered that the people there lived exactly as they had previously lived in their villages. They were organized as they had been before: the village the same and street was the same. That soldier was shaken. Why?

I could not comprehend this. Nineteen years have passed, and they are still saying we are from Bir al-Sabiʻ.

—*Journal of an Ordinary Grief*, p. 32.

The motif of the Dragon Slayer that occurs in so many folktales predates Christianity. The story of al-Khader reviving the dead boy is objective and subjective. Regarding the former, the story belongs to the 'the tales of my family about the place'—that is, they are part of a Palestinian identity connected with the land that goes beyond the historical and touches on the mythical. And the subjective is expressed in the author's identification with the resurrected boy in the story his mother tells about al-Khader; he imagines him to be a shepherd and wants, like him, to be resurrected from the dead.

It is clear that the purpose of including this folkloric material bears on the major political theme in the work: the assertion of an identity based on the land itself, and the living history of that land. Several poles of this identity underlie the historical basis of the text. The first (as mentioned earlier) is the Nakba of 1948, which we encounter in his description of the Jordanian Rusaifa, the city where the great majority of the population consists of descendants of people made refugees by the Nakba and who may never return, though UN General Assembly Resolution 194, passed in 1948, mandates that return.[8] The second pole is the current Israeli occupation that creates wounds in the land

---

8 For information on the Nakba, including a map of the destroyed Palestinian villages, see the website of the Israeli human rights organization that calls for the return of the refugees, Zochrot: https://zochrot.org/

'The United Nations General Assembly adopts resolution 194 (III) resolving that "refugees wishing to return to their homes and live at peace with their neighbours should be permitted to do so at the earliest practicable date, and that compensation should be paid for the property of those choosing not to return and for loss of or damage to property which, under principles of international law or equity, should be made good by the Governments or authorities responsible."'— https://www.unrwa.org/content/resolution-194.

with its settlements and ends up trashing the orchards that Barghouthi grew up in. Barghouthi's description of the landscape is haunting because the action is most often set at night in full moonlight, which is contrasted with the halogen lamps of the Israeli settlement.

In closing, I want to draw attention to the last three lines of the song of the elderly woman in the colourful Palestinian garment: 'May God grant you the stone of the house / And extend the reach of your life / Like the reach of olives into the oil.'[9] Unfortunately, the translation has to sacrifice the rhyme, but the metaphor of the olive reaching into the oil is powerful even without it. The oil is the essence of the olive, and this 'reach' is nature's power, for it is the secret process of growth that takes place outside human knowledge or ability to control, other than to destroy it, as the Israeli setters attempt to do around the time of the harvest each year. Immediately after quoting the poem, Barghouthi says, 'And if the olive can reach into its oil, then the Mountain can reach into its olive trees.'

The reach of the olive into the oil, the reach of the Mountain in its olive trees, the reach of the author into the Paradise of the Pharaohs, the world-wide reach of the Mountain—they are all part of the same 'reach', the reach of the author into the text, and the reach of the text into the reader, and ultimately the reach of the work across time. It is most appropriate that Barghouthi, who loves folktales and thinks of his memoir as one, should choose the folk idea of the olive reaching into the oil as the dominant force

---

9 On the reach of the olive into the oil, compare the opening lines of Dylan Thomas' poem, 'The Force . . .':

> The force that through the green fuse drives the flower /
> Drives my green age . . .

—*Collected Poems*, p. 10.

in this work. He has adopted it as a metaphor for the act of writing, the same mysterious process that takes place in nature itself. Emily Dickinson's poem, 'This Was a Poet,' distils the meaning of this process in its first six lines:

> This was a Poet—It is That
> Distils amazing sense
> From ordinary Meanings—
> And Attar so immense
> From the familiar species
> That perished by the Door.[10]

* * *

Acknowledgements

An invitation from Amal Eqeiq and Samer Al-Saber to give a talk at the event commemorating Hussein Barghouthi's death (held at the University of Washington on 2 May 2011), began the engagement with his works that led to this translation. Many of the ideas from that talk have found their way into the Introduction. I am happy to acknowledge their indirect contribution to this work.

---

10 *Collected Poems*, #448, p. 215.

Attar is the fragrance—the very essence of the rose—just as the oil is the liquid attar of the olive. The word comes the from the Arabic word ʿaṭir ('fragrant'). The olive tree, the heart of Palestine, is a complex symbol whose significance includes history, the land, the people and their history on the land; it is also a source of livelihood for the majority. The trees are under constant threat of being uprooted by Israeli settlers every year around harvest time: 'I turned on the radio to listen to the news. The settlers were burning a mountain of olive trees in a village in the north.' As a result, there is now an international brigade for the protection of the olive harvest.

The native ear of my wife, Jane Muhawi, has always served as the ultimate court of appeal in the battle for nuances.

* * *

Works Cited

BLAKE, William. *The Complete Poems*. London: Longman, Norton Edition, 1977.

DARWISH, Mahmoud. *Ākhir al-Layl* ('The Last Part of Night'), *Al-ʿAṣāfiru Tamūtu fī al-Jalīl* ('The Birds Are Dying in Galilee') and *Uḥibbuki Aw Lā Uḥibbuki* ('I Love You, Or I Love You Not). *Collected Works*, VOL. 1. Beirut: Dar al-Awda, 1994.

———. *Arā Mā Urīd* ('I See What I Want'). *Collected Works*, VOL. 2. Beirut: Dar al-Awda, 1994.

———. *Why Did You Leave the Horse Alone?* (Jeffrey Sacks trans.). Brooklyn, NY: Archipelago Books, 2006.

———. *Jidārīya: Qaṣīda* ('Mural: An Ode') in *If I Were Another* (Fady Joudah trans.). New York: Farrar, Straus, and Giroux, 2009.

———. *Journal of an Ordinary Grief* (Ibrahim Muhawi trans.). Brooklyn, NY: Archipelago Books, 2010.

DAVIS, Rochelle. *Palestine Village Histories: Geographies of the Displaced*. Stanford, CA: Stanford University Press, 2011.

DICKINSON, Emily. *Collected Poems* (Thomas H. Johnson ed.). Boston: Little, Brown, 1956.

ELIOT, T. S. *The Wasteland: And Other Poems*. London: Faber and Faber, 1999.

ERNST, Carl W. *Words of Ecstasy in Sufism*. Albany: State University of New York Press, 1985.

HANAUER, J. E. *Folklore of the Holy Land: Moslem, Christian, and Jewish*. London: Sheldon, 1935. Available at: www.sacred-texts.com/asia/flhl/flhl12.htm

KHALIDI, Tarif. *The Qur'an: A New Translation*. New York: Penguin Books, 2009.

KHALIDI, Walid. *Before Their Diaspora: A Photographic history of the Palestinians, 1876–1948*. Washington, DC: Institute for Palestine Studies, 1984.

LORCA, Federico García. *Poem of the Deep Song* (Carlos Bauer trans.). San Francisco: City Lights Books, 1987.

MASALHA, Nur. *The Palestine Nakba: Decolonising History, Narrating the Subaltern, Reclaiming Memory*. London: Zed Books, 2012.

MUHAWI, Ibrahim and Sharif Kanaana. *Speak, Bird, Speak Again: Palestinian Arab Folktales*. Berkeley: University of California Press, 1989.

NIETZSCHE, Friederich. *The Portable Nietzsche* (Walter Kaufman, ed. and trans.). London: Penguin Books, 1982.

PAPPÉ, Ilan. *The Ethnic Cleansing of Palestine*. London: Oneworld, 2006. Available online at: https://yplus.ps/wp-content/uploads/2021/01/Pappe-Ilan-The-Ethnic-Cleansing-of-Palestine.pdf.

SHAKESPEARE, William. *A Casebook on Shakespeare's Sonnets* (Gerald Willen and Victor B. Reed eds). New York: Thomas Y. Crowell, 1962.

SHAWQI, Ahmad. *Maṣra' Kiliobatrā* ('The Death of Cleopatra'). Available online at: https://ggle.io/4QfU

THOMAS, Dylan. Collected Poems. New York: New Directions, 1957.

YEATS, William Butler. *The Collected Poems*. New York: Macmillan, 1960.

A NOTE ON THE TRANSLATION

Al-Deir al-Juwwānī. The word deir, when used with reference to a ruin, designates a Byzantine monastery; the author makes mention of this fact indirectly later in the memoir, where he also provides an impressionistic explanation for the meaning of the word *inner* (juwwānī). An indication of the number of monasteries that once existed in Palestine is the large number of towns and villages—before 1948 and after—that have a name beginning with Deir, including the village of Deir Ghassaneh (the ancestral home of the Barghouthis). The deir referred to in the memoir sits atop a mountain at a distance from the village of Kobar, where the author was born on 5 May 1954. It is where he returned later in life after many years of 'voluntary exile', and where he died (1 May 2002) and was buried in the almond-tree orchard by the house.

I use the Arabic originals for words that can be found in English dictionaries, like keffiyeh and aba (men's garment in Palestine, though used with reference to women's outer cloak in other Arab countries), without diacritical marks. I have also left names the way they are generally known—thus Feiruz, not Fairūz; Mahmoud Darwish, not Maḥmūd Darwīsh; and the Qur'an, rather than the Qur'ān. The only exception is the name of the author's son, Áthar, for which I have adopted his own spelling as we see it on the Internet in his biographical tribute to his father, written in English. The stress on the first letter is necessary—without it, the complex meaning of the name would change to the univocal 'trace'. There is a longish reflection by the author on names in general and why he chose this particular one for his son, and there are explanations in the Notes for the linguistic complexities surrounding this choice.

In the Notes, on the other hand, all Arabic quotations are transliterated according to the system recommended by the Library of Congress. Hence, the difference between deir in the text, which is how the word is pronounced in the spoken Arabic of Palestine, and its Modern Standard Arabic equivalent—al-Dayr—in the Notes. The author uses the word jabal ('mountain') for the steep hills of central Palestine, and I have stayed with it, because it is current in the country. Compare 'Mount of Olives', 'Mount Carmel', 'Mount of Temptation'.

Barghouthi's text is in poetic prose—elegant but not affected. The translation was guided by his style in order to convey the uniqueness of the writing without sacrificing fluency. As is well known, Arabic is a diglossic language, meaning that in addition to the Modern Standard, there are local spoken varieties. All the popular songs that the author cites or quotes, whether his own or the numerous quotations from Feiruz's songs, are in the vernacular Arabic of Palestine and Lebanon.

We should take note of the choices I made regarding the frequently occurring word khurrafiyya, which I have translated as 'folktale' or 'fairy tale', depending on the context. We also find the word ḥikāya, meaning simple 'tale', in the title of the second chapter ('Land of Tales') and other places. Two words in Arabic designate a folk narrative: ḥikāya (tale) and khurrafiya and both designate oral tales told by the older women in local Arabic to female members and children in an extended family setting, as discussed in *Speak, Bird, Speak Again: Palestinian Arab Folktales.* These are the tales that his mother tells him as a child, tales of the jinn and the ghouls. They include local legends, like that about the Qteliya Spring, personal narratives that he tells about his mother, his aunt and his ancestors, jinn stories, stories about the Inner Monastery and the lives of his ancestors therein. Many Palestinian, and general Arab folktales include magical, or supernatural, elements, like or the jinn, or sub-human elements, like the ghouls and ghoulas, that we find here in abundance. A possible source of confusion for the reader may lie in the manner in which the author interweaves the imaginative world of folktales and the landscape where the memoir is set and the animals he encounters in it.

Fairy tales on the other hand, are literary productions, re-writings of oral folktales in the standard language—a trend that began with Charles Perrault and his circle in seventeenth-century France. With the gradual disappearance of oral traditions, current usage has tended to group these words together, as we can see in the names of standard reference works, such as *Folktales and Fairy tales: Traditions and Texts from around the World,* and *The Greenwood Encyclopedia of Folktales and Fairy Tales.* With current practice in mind, I did not always use my preference (folktale), but have used it interchangeably with *fairy tale* when the context called for it. The author also describes customs and traditions that have disappeared from Palestinian folk life, like the Thursday of the Dead, the material culture associated with it, and the preparations made for it.

Regarding spelling: contractions are used only in dialogue, for which a less formal tone is adopted. The author relies more extensively on quotation marks in his text than would be appropriate for prose in English. I have kept them only when their purpose was obvious, as in drawing attention to something immediately at hand, or when they seem to be quotations from sources that I cannot locate. Poetry citations that are not annotated are presumably from his own songs.

The written form of the author's last name is Al-Barghouthi, but it is almost always Barghouti, without the definite article and with 't' instead of 'th' at the end. Barghouthi is the name of the largest family in Palestine, and the English spelling of the name that one finds on the internet or in books varies from one person to another. In considering which form to follow here, I decided that my best guide would be the way his son Áthar spells it in English, Barghouthi, without the definite article. The best-known literary Barghouthis now are the poets Mourid Barghouti (1944–2021, author of two journals of Palestinian exile, *I Saw Ramallah,* and *I Was Born There, I Was Born Here*), his son Tamim Al Barghouti, and our author.

The Notes serve the obvious purpose of opening out the text for the English-language reader. They provide sources and explain obscurities. It was fortunate that most of the information I needed was available on the Internet. Ordinary Arab readers may not necessarily know much about Mahmoud Darwish's poetry (though he is probably the most cited poet on social media), but everyone knows the songs of Feiruz. She is called the Lady of Lebanese songs, and her popularity is such that all her music is available on the Internet. (The same is true of nearly all of Darwish.) The songs speak in ways that the text cannot articulate: they *add* an aesthetic dimension to the text and extend its domain into popular culture.

Regarding gender : Arabic is already a gendered language, but in places where one would try to be gender-correct I have translated the text as it is, without attempting to fit it into the correct sexual politics prevalent in English writing (though I do so in my Introduction).

Unless otherwise noted, all translations are by me, except those from the Qur'an, whose source is *The Qur'an: A New Translation* by Tarif Khalidi.

AMONG THE
ALMOND TREES

CHAPTER ONE

The 'Inner Monastery'

After an absence of thirty years I have returned to live in the countryside near Ramallah—'returned to the beauty that had been betrayed'. I had exiled myself from my beginnings and chosen to live as an expatriate. I am one who has perfected 'beginnings' but not 'endings'. My return, therefore, is an imperfect 'ending'.

The moon was full and the air freezing as I walked among the shadows of the almond trees in the orchards around our house, contemplating this 'ending'. What had made me come back was the disease of cancer, and the pain in my lower back that was unceasing to the point of tedium. And boredom, as Kierkegaard said, 'is so terrifying that I cannot but say it is terrifying to the point of boredom'. My illness has now come to define my outlook on life.

There was no room for me in the action of the Intifada, except to haunt the Ramallah hospital, as it has now become my Kaaba, or my last Wailing Wall. Here there is room for me between the new births on the upper floor and the morgue refrigerator below. I am infirm, wandering around on the outskirts of things, on the edge of what is happening. For example, in the hospital's strange hallways, inhabited by beings with green caps and green gowns, a pathologist walks behind gurneys for anaesthetized people who have not woken up, or will never awaken. At the emergency entrance is a bottleneck of ambulances, each marked with a red crescent, like the one I used to see in the sky behind the mountains. All around me are the martyred and the wounded. I roam the hallways, asking about the haematologist. 'We're in a situation of emergency,' a nurse answers nervously, 'Can't you see?' Then I realize I am a superfluous person, an obtrusive sick man moving towards his destiny, alone with his worries. I'm not a visitor here, nor a healthy person, nor a wounded youth, nor a martyr. I'm an 'ordinary sick person', an expression caught between the dictionary of the living and the dead—between the new births on the upper floor and the morgue on the lower. What should a human being feel who can observe what is going on but is forbidden from 'interfering', and whose nose is filled with the smell of medicines rather than saffron? How should he feel, caught between these two floors?

That is what made me return to the countryside, to a beauty that I had betrayed before—a return whose plot had not been perfected.

I had planned my return for a long time, especially my night-time visit to the mountains of my childhood. The moon was full and the silence complete amid the ruins of the ancient monastery at the summit of a mountain far from the village. I stood there, contemplating beginnings and endings. Suddenly something strange indeed occurred. I heard what sounded exactly like a small child crying in the depths of the moonlit fig and olive orchards. My hair stood on end. I peered into the heart of the darkness, past the pale boulders, but saw no one. The sound seemed to have come from an invisible creature in the broad fields.

Stunned and alarmed, I cautiously moved forward. The crying did not stop; instead, the closer I drew, the further it seemed to go. I hurried, but still could not reach it. I crossed many orchards, but it stayed the same distance away. I returned to where I had begun, thinking that these mountains must be inhabited by the jinn, the very air filled with madness. Or, they were simply different. Yet the sound followed me, and even came so close that I felt afraid. I reached for a stick and turned in its direction, but could see nothing other than small trees in the moonlight. I was in the front orchard, but when I thought I had reached it, the sound seemed to be coming from the next. I was utterly baffled. I thought it might be a hyena, but the sound of the hyena is not so delicate nor so filled with sadness, so childlike and otherworldly. Yet, what else could it be? Hyenas are afraid of fire, and attack solitary people like me. They spray urine on the face of their victims, so as to stun them. I pulled out a box of matches from my pocket and headed back in the direction of the monastery ruins. Then I stood there, thinking.

My mother was an orphan, and for a time had danced and sung at the festivals of the local fellahin. She was adopted by an uncle called Qaddura, a giant of a man, quite robust. He lived with his brother, I believe, in this very monastery. They were armed robbers. Whenever a cow or a mare disappeared, everyone said it was at the monastery, where no one dared to go. One moonlit night, as he was riding his donkey back home, a 'rogue' snake struck Qaddura's right foot. He leapt off at once, and jumped about until the snake withdrew its fangs. By the time he arrived at the monastery, he was exhausted, and may have died right where I am standing at this moment. When I was a child, my mother swore she'd seen that 'rogue' snake flying over the moonlit mountains, trilling with joy for having killed Qaddura. The

'Qasaba Snake' had horns like an old bull, she told me, and its hiss made the dry shrubs shiver.

The notion of the 'memory of place' came to mind as I stood there among the ruins. To the west, at the summit of a mountain covered with a forest of pine, cypress and oak, shine the bright halogen lights of the settlement that the Israelis call Halamish and we, the 'Nabi Saleh Settlement'. Cold floodlights and barbed wire everywhere. The settlement seems to be afloat in space, perhaps because of the bright lights, as though it hasn't yet touched land or history. What does a settler from Russia or Estonia, who arrived perhaps no longer than a year ago, see when he opens his window and gazes at these mountains where I am now standing? What will he see and comprehend of these mountains, floating over the history out of which they have risen? He will certainly not see the snake that flies and trills, hear its cry, nor learn the secret that urges the one suffering from cancer to go wandering among the ruins at one o'clock in the morning. He will not touch history even if he were a soothsayer; not my history anyway, even if he were a god.

As I stood there among those ruins, I felt there was an enormous difference between the two kinds of light: moonlight, and the halogen light flooding out of the settlement. The latter is focused and oppressive, its glare extreme, reaching even beyond the barbed wire that isolates every such settlement from its environment. It is more like an 'armed vision', an occupation by means of vision, and the visual architect of a state in the delirium of armed visions lit by halogens even in its sleep. The settlement as a whole seems like a book about the soul, or about the relationship between light and power. No one has yet studied the relation between light and power.

It seemed I was seeing two memories side by side: the memory of snakes that trill with joy as they fly, and a memory made of visions and armed myths that dream of eradicating the snakes. (Didn't Yitzhak Shamir, previous Israeli prime minister, say 'The Arabs are snakes?') Between the two memories, the executioner's and the victim's, is a valley or an abyss, a chasm of some sort, and I am standing on its invisible edge. Could it be that the strange sound like the crying of a small child in this moonlit night was coming from the depths of that chasm?

When I returned home, I asked an uncle, who was older and had a greater store of memory, about the sound. 'That's the sound of a small animal called ghreriya. In the old days, they used to hunt it with dogs and shotguns. Its meat is delicious, but now it's extinct. You might have heard the last ghreriya in the mountains.' 'They're not extinct,' I thought, 'There were ghreriyas at the Ramallah hospital too. They were giving birth or being born on the upper floor. Or being preserved in the morgue refrigerator below. Indeed, I have seen them.'

I had formed a deep attachment to the Inner Monastery, as if captivated by the very act of standing in the path of what blew there from my ancestors' memories in order to construct my beginnings from their endings. For example, I would try to imagine my mother's uncle Qaddura playing his rabab as he stood on the roof, looking out onto the deep, moonlit valleys and terraced orchards that had been ploughed and planted. My mother swore that people heard him all the way over not only in the neighbouring villages but also in the distant ones. I imagined him hanging a shotgun on each of the Monastery's four walls, climbing the narrow stone steps, spreading his cloak on the ground and starting to play. I do not like the rabab, I prefer the nay. Then I try to imagine that highwayman playing the nay.

They say that reeds hold a divine secret that God (All praise to Him!) had planted in the breast of Prophet Muhammad. Unable to bear it, the Prophet revealed the secret to Ali Ibn Abi Taleb, and entreated him to not tell anyone. But Ali could not bear it either, so he went to a deep and distant valley and revealed it to the reeds. From that day on, the sound of every nay made out of reeds sets free a divine secret that cannot be spoken in words. The sadness of the nay, Mevlana Jaluluddin Rumi tells us, is the yearning of the reed for the plant from which it was cut, its origin, its first valley.

For what origin did our Qaddura yearn, which beginnings?

* * *

From the roof of the Monastery where he played his instrument, Qaddura could almost see Deir Ghassaneh, the native village of the Barghouthi tribe, and his as well. His ancestors came from there—at least his the ones he knew of did.

Once, there was a feud among the elders of the tribe, and on a moonlit night like tonight, my great-grandfather stole into a house and killed twelve of his male relatives while they slept. Then he packed his horses and camels, his women and children, and ran away to this distant spot where, a century and a half later, I would be born from such a 'beginning'.

Qaddura belonged to that fugitive lineage. He had four brothers, the same number as the shotguns that hung on his four walls. Kayid, the most powerful among them, lived with him at the Monastery.

One night, Kayid, riding his white stallion, chanced to pass the clan hall where the elders spent their evenings. As he rode past, he saw Qaddura emerge, fuming with anger because one of the elders had interrupted him when he was speaking. Kayid got off his horse, strode into the hall, and, grabbing the elder by his shirt, said, 'Your horns have grown big since I've been away. I'll have to break them for you.' He was Qaddura's right arm. One time, he used ropes to climb up into a mansion of an important elder. He managed to unlock the doors and was about to lead away the horses and the cattle, but the guards woke up and caught him and held him prisoner. When news of this reached the Monastery, his sister said, 'Don't worry about him—worry about what's going to happen to the mansion.' Qaddura sent a letter, warning the elder to release Kayid in three days.

Three days later, Kayid was back home.

It was to be expected that Kayid's funeral would be special. The evening that news of his death reached our village, a group of men and women headed for the roofs and courtyards, each holding a stick wrapped with a cloth dipped in olive oil or tar. They lit up their torches and danced the night away in celebration of his passing.

As for Qaddura, he lived for a while until he died from the bite of the trilling snake. Three females' under his protection were rendered homeless: his wife, my mother and his rabab.

His wife was addicted to snuff and acquired the nickname 'Snuffie'. She left the Monastery, which then fell into ruin, and moved to the village, to an old Crusader-style stone house. Its door was made of heavy wood, and the walls and the roof formed a single stone arch. When I was a child, the house seemed to me an endless tunnel. My mother sometimes sent me to sleep there, at Snuffie's house. One night, I suddenly woke up. The lantern was still shining, its pale yellow light radiating through that bizarre house that felt like a strange and warm womb. Snuffie was panting, sniffing her snuff and muttering invocations and obscure spells.

They say that the embryo hears the sound of the blood circu-
lating in the womb like the roll of the ocean, and that, after being
born, the baby falls asleep to any sound resembling that embry-
onic rumble—our very first rhythm. I used to hear that rhythm
in her voice, and the fluttering of the lantern's flame seemed to
deepen it somehow. She stood there like the first mother, like
Mother Earth. Tied round her head was a head covering with
faded colours, adorned with chains of Ottoman coins that rattled
every time she moved. Across her chin and wide lips was a tattoo,
its green so dark it was almost blue. She walked slowly towards
the door, then towards the lantern, then stood there, rapt in
thought. Outside, it was raining and windy.

After the death of Qaddura, she became the village midwife.
They would come for her, even on nights like this. She would heat
water in a copper kettle on the brazier and mutter prayers about
a thoroughbred mare that would rise safely—and then pull the
new-born out of its mother's womb. How I tried to understand
those nights of new births and the role that Snuffie played in each
of them, and how she made a living from that very ancient pro-
fession. In birth there is an enigma, like the womb and the mother
and the emotions of Snuffie herself.

Snuffie's end was humiliating because her only daughter had
put her in an old- people's home in Ramallah. Though it was only
for two weeks, something seemed to break in her soul. She died
soon after she came home, and her Crusader-style house was
closed up forever, until it also collapsed.

As for my mother, she too left the Inner Monastery and came
to live under the protection of relatives who did not have
Qaddura's manliness or his generosity of spirit. Once she told me
that God had built a wall around her heart, and that she could
have feelings for no one in those days, or perhaps she said, 'from

that time.' My father loved her, a man with the same ancestry as Qaddura, from the same stock, perhaps even with the same family curse. He wanted to marry her. When her relatives turned him down, he called a friend of his, Yahya, and they sat at the threshold of the house, each with a shotgun in his lap. They said they were going to kill any man who 'granted himself the right to marry her.' After he finally won her hand, they travelled to Amman for their honeymoon, and when they came back, he planted the orchards around our house with almond trees for her.

After some decades, Yahya ended up as a truck driver on the desert route between Jordan and Kuwait, where the temperature rises to forty-five degrees centigrade in the shade. A straight road that goes on forever.

He used to place a small rock on the accelerator, secure the steering wheel in place with a string and let the truck drive on by itself. One day they found him dead in his truck as it rolled on, on its own, perhaps in the direction of the oil fields.

* * *

Qaddura did not fully die when the rogue viper bit him. He left behind his rabab. I can still hear its echoes in the space separating my beginning from his end. I wish I could produce a film that I would then title *The Life Story of a Rabab*.

My father inherited the rabab from him, and, till 1948, played it whenever he sang. After that he never sang again, and never said a word that even hinted he had any feelings for music. He behaved as if he had completely forgotten his voice. He gave away the rabab to one of his brothers, famous for his silence. That uncle of mine always sat cross-legged in front of his house, his gaze turned towards the mountains, and soon acquired a reputation for his sharp vision. If a mare wandered away, he would say, 'Look for her in such-and-such a place.' And if someone's distant vegetable crop was being nibbled on by a gazelle, he could see that too.

They say he had one of the most beautiful voices in the entire district of Ramallah, but had, for unknown reasons, chosen silence. Once I asked him about the happiest days of his life, and he said, 'When I was a child, playing with my cap in the dirt.' Qaddura's rabab rusted under his care, and its string grew loose from the never-ending silence. In forty years, I only heard him sing once, and only for a moment, at the wedding of his son.

That night, a huge lamp lit up our clan guesthouse—the air was thick with happiness and the aroma of Arabic coffee. Women's songs wafted out of a house nearby. Everyone was happy, except for him. It was as if there resided in him a force that had been raised to resist happiness. He sat centre-stage in the guesthouse with a dignity suitable to his age, wearing a mustard-coloured abah, a black headband around his kufiya, his eyes silently wandering over the guests as though he were surveying another expanse of the mountains. Suddenly everyone fell quiet—if a needle had fallen to the floor, its clink would have been heard. Then one of the elders stood up, approached him and begged him for God's sake and his son's wedding to sing something. I was sitting near him, and watched a tremor ripple across his cheeks. He closed his eyes for a while, and then I heard a voice the like of which I had never heard again:

They bring me the arak, white in the glass
And now that my head is grey, 'Rejoice!' they say

He did not finish. No one broke the silence to say, 'Carry on!'

* * *

And silence is music. This is ancient wisdom, but few know that there are different kinds of silence. The silence of the Monastery on a moonlit night with frost in the air is strange indeed. In front of a cave with a small rectangular door, dating back to the Roman era, for example, there used to be a basin into which had settled water and skulls from huge crumbling structures. Grave robbers had demolished the cave in search of gold. I arrived there by a short path that ran through a wood filled with pine trees, cypresses and wild thyme. Silence all around, the moon shining in the sky and a mild breeze shaking the top of a pine tree. Suddenly I heard a sneezing, a faint, subdued sneezing, but not from a human or a jinn. As it drew closer, I stopped in my tracks, uncertain. And in a moment that flashed faster than a dream I saw a herd of gazelle crossing the path. They were leaping—and sneezing. Each gazelle suspended in space for a moment, then dropping to the ground. It was as if I had seen among the dark trees a herd of obscure shadows that almost broke into song. Then a fearful silence set in, as though nothing had taken place—a silence that was like the passing of an enormous span of time during which a beauty had its day and then perished.

I stood there stunned, like someone on whose head a bird had landed. Then it occurred to me that a gazelle hunter had set a trap for them—and for me—of the kind that could crack even a thigh bone, and that I might get caught in it. Or that a hyena had caused the gazelles to bolt, and was now lying in wait behind a rock or a tree.

Nothing comes to the surface in solitude except that which is already deep within us. I suddenly became aware of many fears. In front of me was a meadow, ploughed and moonlit, reaching all the way to the wall of the Monastery. And a human being, any human being, is afraid of emptiness. I was afraid to enter the meadow that was exposed from every direction. There were some olive saplings that looked like faint shadows, like ancient monks in their dark habits, singing with raised hands to the 'Dweller on High':

From this broad meadow
Our hands are raised
Like the tall trees

There is a special spiritual energy that wells up from this spot, and if I were to lose my concentration, or fall sleep, the latent 'powers of the place' will awaken, and everything in it, including the stones, will come back to life.

As if in a trance, on the edge between waking and dreaming, magic and reality, I entered the meadow into fields of total silence, the kind of silence that is only to be found here. I did not want anyone to accompany me, because a human being can draw the attention of others to himself. I wanted to walk through here, forgotten, paying attention to no one and no one paying attention to me, in order to face my fears on my own.

When I reached the door of the cave, I stopped. I felt as though the skulls of many generations were rolling under the threshold. And I felt that a human being was a light shadow, moonlit and swinging between two powers: the power of skeletons scattered about in a stone basin from the time of the Romans, and a power that raises him to higher ground, like the cypress and pine trees and the gazelle and wild thyme. Around him, in this meadow of shadows, in the middle of all this, grows the wisdom of foxes. A wisdom that, as Mahmoud Darwish said, cries out, 'Live for your body, not your illusions; live for you flesh, not your dream!'

I was exhausted. Cancer is a view of two mountains: the mountain of flesh to the west, and the mountain of dreams to the east, the mountain of the body under and that of illusions above. I raised my hands in order to look like an olive tree, and not a cave. And maybe I looked ridiculous. Nevertheless this was no dream or illusion or prayer, for there is no sky closer to the earth than the sky above the Monastery on the Mountain?

The sky here is near
And will listen to us, my darling

In us, in all of us, there is strength beyond the body. Afterwards, I sat on the wall of the Monastery in front of the meadow, but as Mevlana Jalaluddin Rumi said: 'I will not sit here to count blessings not understood by mathematics.'

The meadow by moonlight was as white as salt, almost as transparent as lunar crystals that cannot hide what is inside them. I thought I saw a road running through that meadow and branching out into three paths, as in the folktales of my people: 'the path of clarity', 'the path of uncertainty' and 'the path of no-return'.

My mother used to say that the ghūla would sit at the crossing of three paths and light up 'the ghūla's lantern' (an insect with a luminous phosphorus tip on its head that would fly about at night, looking like an errant lamp, or one of the 'eyes of the place'). To tempt travellers and passers-by, the ghūla' would grind salt, with her breasts thrown over her shoulders. And she will die if you strike her with the sword once, but if you strike twice she will come back to life. And if she says to you, 'Strike again!' you must say, 'My mother didn't teach me how.' This was the advice of my mother to her little prince who at that time did not own anything but a wooden sword.

Yet, what path did I take in my beginnings? Not 'the path of clarity', for I lived like a man who had lost his way for thirty years; nor 'the path of no-return', for I have come back to the Monastery. Consequently, I have taken 'the path of uncertainty'.

* * *

And demolition is an ant!

As a child, I used to envy the shepherds their freedom and their wildernesses, and dreamt of being a shepherd of geese, partridge or gazelles. The reason for this wish was my mother's tale about a prince who owned a castle in which there was everything the heart could desire. He had livestock and chickens and dovecotes, but he was a miser. One day, two strangers on horses came by. They were Lord Khader the Green and Lord Jesus. The prince was too cheap to offer them any of his sheep or fowl; so he slaughtered a child under his protection, cooked him in yoghurt sauce and offered him to them on a platter. Lord Khader then rose and said, 'Rise, slaughtered boy in the yoghurt sauce!' The cooked meat trembled, and the child slowly rose up in front of them. Lord Khader then called upon God (May he be praised and exalted!) to change all the prince's sheep into gazelles, all his chickens into wild quail and all his turkeys into mountain geese. And thus it was. From the moment the child was slaughtered, night fell over the earth. The light of day returned only after his resurrection. And I imagined that child, whose destiny 'the tales of my family about the place' had left vague, to be a shepherd of geese, or gazelles, or wild pigeons. I wanted to live with him. And because my dream was impossible, I became fond of going along with those who resemble him—the shepherds.

I pressed my mother until she bought me an ewe lamb that was red in colour. She turned out to be a devil, and quicker than any gazelle. Using the excuse of taking her to pasture, I became friends with the owner of the biggest herd in the mountains. Ali the shepherd accepted me because, even though I owned only one red sheep, I tended his whole herd. We used to leave the village early in the morning, when the air was cold and the dew still frozen and glittering on the grass like specks of snow. At high noon—and that, by shepherd reckoning, was when the shadow of a stick planted in the ground was at its shortest reach, almost disappearing into the stick itself—we would lead the herd to the Qteiliya.

The Qteiliya was a spring about an hour's walk to the south of the Monastery. It gushed out of a crack at the bottom of a huge rock that nothing could climb except blackberries, oaks or a small dog. All around it were irrigated orchards with all that was desirable of fruit, each according to its season—peaches, apples and apricots, to name only a few. I would lie down in the shadows on top of the rocks, close my eyes and listen to the bubbling of the spring as it poured into a natural pool before it was channelled into the orchards. Ali would sit under the carob tree, playing the nay with his mouth, but without an actual nay. I thought that was amazing.

Ali was a dark-complexioned young man, tanned by the sun. His body was as taut as a gazelle. He knew the fragrance and flavour of every plant in the mountains, for he hailed from a lineage of shepherds from the time of the Stone Age, when animals were first domesticated in this region. He would milk the sheep in an aluminium pan and squeeze into it some drops of fig milk (a sour white liquid that exudes from the root of unripe figs), and the milk would then clot into a delicious cheese with the flavour of figs.

Ali knew only the wilderness. Even the names of his brothers and sisters were those of birds: 'He-bird' and 'She-bird'. And he loved three things: the shotgun, the nay and dogs. Every aspect of his life had a ritual. For example, he would steal a dog when it was still a puppy. He would then cut off its ears and tail, and sterilize the wounds with vinegar, lemon juice and herbs. 'If the dog were to fight with a wolf, a hyena or another dog, they can take hold of it by the ears, or the tail. It is better for it to have none.' The dog would be taught two things: absolute violence, and obedience. When he whistled once, the dog would snap at anyone or anything that Ali pointed to; another whistle, and the dog would lie down at his feet like a lamb.

One day, he said he was going to prepare a feast for me. He made bait from a grain of wheat that he soaked in water until it was swollen with moisture. He then threaded it on a string, and created something that looked like a fishhook. Early next morning, he spied a hen in the neighbourhood. He threw the grain of wheat in front of it—and it swallowed the bait. Then Ali pulled it behind him with the string. The hen could do nothing; it could not spit out the grain of wheat from its gullet nor save itself from the string. Nor could it cackle. In the evening, by the spring, he roasted it on the fire.

The moon that night was a red disc rising from behind the distant wadis. The animals wandered about here or there, or dozed in the shadows. I took off my clothes and went into the pool for a swim, and Ali played the nay with his mouth. Suddenly he said that I was swimming in a pool of tears! He said that long ago, before he was born, there was a beautiful woman who was killed by her family. The wronged woman transformed into a houri and began to haunt this spring, which came to be known as Ein al-Qatila or 'Spring of the Woman Who Was Killed'. I imagined the crack from which the water sprang as the eye of a weeping houri whose tears formed this big pool, then branched out to irrigate the orchards all around us.

On account of the moonlight, the shadows in the orchards sparked various fears. Ali played an unfamiliar tune with his mouth, and the wadi seemed a twisting path that emitted light, like the Milky Way. As for the mountain, it looked like a woman sleeping in the light of the moon. Shotgun in hand, Ali stood on a rock near the carob tree, as if he had smelt a wolf or a hyena. He called the dogs, and they ran over and stood by him. Then he fell silent. A special and complete silence, except for the chirping of the crickets under the carob trees and in the wadi.

I remembered a story my father had told me, about a merchant who sold peaches and apricots loaded on his donkey. He used to cross the mountains with his donkey, to go to Haifa and Jaffa, and then return. One night, on his way back from Jaffa, laden with tins of kerosene, a hyena started to harass his donkey. Every time the hyena rubbed its body against the donkey, the merchant splashed it with kerosene. Finally, he lit a match and threw it. At once the hyena burst into flames and began running through the orchards like a crazed torch, blazing a trail of fire everywhere it went. The hyena is the legend of the Mountain. It is said that when a hyena takes away the mind of a lone, wandering man, he follows it, crying 'Yaba! Yaba! Father! Father!' It seems that a moment comes when the father turns into a hyena, and the hyena into a father. Whoever is touched by that moment is said to be 'possessed by the hyena'. The possessed person then follows his 'father', and does not regain his senses until he reaches the entrance to the hyena's lair. When his forehead collides with the top of the entrance, blood begins to flow down on his face, and only then does he realize that he has been following a hyena and not his father. So whenever a person is late, people would tend to say, 'A hyena has devoured him.'

It is not strange, then, that the shepherd should stand on the rock and whistle to his dogs, rifle in hand. Ali the shepherd, like the snake that trills as it flies, or the hyena, is a son of this mountain, made from the same soil. He is like a sad nay tune, and bears on his skin the scent of these desolate wilds.

I grew up and left Ali the shepherd to the wilds, and never asked about him, not once, till I fell ill with cancer and started to sneak back into the mountains of my childhood—the 'beauty that had been betrayed'—in preparation for life in the countryside around Ramallah. I was told that Israeli Security had bought him two hunting dogs in Tel Aviv, and thus used his primitive and instinctive love of dogs to charm its way into his heart. He never realized that a dog too could serve as bait, just like a swollen grain of wheat. One night, just before this intifada, one of his relatives had knocked on his door. They used to spend their evenings together, so Ali had no doubts about opening the door and walking out, only to be surprised with a heavy calibre revolver—that of his son, in fact—touching his temple and then making his head explode with a single bullet, because he was a 'spy'.

I know the young man who assassinated him. He used to come to our house in Birzeit, and spend his evenings with me. He did not realize he had also killed a spot in the memory of the child I had been. Should I kneel before the victim and embrace the killer, as Father Zossima does in *The Brothers Karamazov*, or should I return secretly to the moonlit mountains of my childhood but keep away from the places in which at one time I was a 'shepherd' and a child?

The Israelis confiscated my childhood—the mountains surrounding the Spring of the Qteiliya—in any case. Over the mountain in whose spring I used to swim while Ali the shepherd stood under his carob tree, they built a settlement lit with floodlights and surrounded by barbed wire. 'The mountain! O Sariya, the mountain!'. It was as if the memory exploded inside me instead of my having to bring it to mind. I started to avoid the places of my childhood. All that remained for me was the Monastery.

At the Ramallah hospital, when I was lost and wandering, looking for the haematologist and watching the gurneys with the anesthetized patients who had not yet woken up, or those who will never awaken, come and go, my mind like a head full of white clouds from the drugs, a stranger hugged me. 'Do you remember me?'

'Sorry. No.'

'Do you remember the Spring of the Qteiliya?'

'Yes.'

'Do you remember a young boy like you who used to guard the orchards and swim with you while Ali the shepherd played the nay? I am he. The son of the owner of the orchards.'

'And the orchards?'

'The settlers started to come down from the top of the mountain and fire their rifles at us. They cut a dirt road from the settlement to the wadi. We ran away, and never went back. And the orchards have turned into banquets for the ruins!'

Demolition is an ant. That is certain.

As I said, my father had planted the gardens around our house with almond trees in 1948, the year of his marriage. Among the moonlit shadows of the almond trees, my back was writhing like a snake from the pain. I have started to forget. Oh, God, how I have started to forget! One night, I noticed that the almond trees were beginning to bloom. The blossoms looked like white butterflies being born from the moonlight. Before Islam, the Arabs used to believe that a woman who exposed her nakedness to the light of the moon could be impregnated by it. Consequently, women used to circumambulate the Kaaba during the season of the hajj wearing no clothes. Covering their private parts with their hands, they sang:

Today, part of it, or all, may show
But remains forbidden what might show

To me, every almond tree is a naked woman in a season of pagan hajj. I peered at the butterflies, feeling certain, for some strange reason, that they were born to reveal an old secret, perhaps one of my earliest secrets, perhaps a pagan one.

Once my mother said to me, 'If you can't keep a secret, dig a hole in the ground and tell it the secret. Then pile dirt on it. Bury it in that hole. It will come back to you when spring comes: every blade of grass or a narcissus that comes up will bring the secret back to the surface. No one will be able to hear that secret except you.' I stood in the middle of the orchards and tried to remember which secret I had buried, in which hole, and wondered which plant would bring it back to me.

There is a dry and parched almond tree that is nothing more than a dark trunk with two branches stretching up to the wide moonlit sky. The shape of that trunk awakened in me a strange feeling, or perhaps an old intuition, about an old secret. A cat that was no less strange than that trunk usually accompanied me on my walks: speckled with black and white spots, as though the spots echoed the trunk that branched into two colours. Its strangeness came from the way it walked. It walked between my legs until I tripped. When I occasionally stepped on its tail, it jumped high and meowed. Yet when I tried to stroke its fur, it ran away, but I couldn't tell into which of its seven souls. In the stories my people tell, cats have seven souls, hiding instincts of the wild that mistrust people. It would run in front of me a metre or two, then lie on its stomach and roll over a number of times while looking up at me. I believed it had something to say to me with movement rather than with words, and with meowing rather than in any of the prevalent languages. One night it jumped up and climbed the dry trunk that resembled an abstract painting in three dimensions. It stood on the tip of the right branch and looked down in my direction, and then up at the moon. And then it froze completely, turning into a statue.

I turned my eyes away, trying to think of what it was trying to say to me. I noticed that the almonds had begun to blossom. I touched the blossoms, smelt them. And I felt that I too would blossom some day.

My mother used to come out to where I was in the shadows of the almond trees. She would ask, 'How is your health?' because she was convinced that I was hiding my illness from her. That night when she asked, 'How is your health?' I answered that the almond trees had begun to blossom. I was amazed when she pointed to the almond tree near the cistern and said, 'This one is the first to blossom.'

'Why?'

'Your father planted these orchards with almond trees the year of our marriage. I was not feeling at home in my new house. So I went to the "Inner Monastery" and brought back one almond kernel and planted it here. And that's the first one to blossom.'

It seems that Qaddura's memory, that is, my mother's old memory, is what blossoms first in her new memory. Without memory, a human being is only the remnant of a human being.

* * *

Morning came, and it was sunny and lazy, with a bite of cold in it. I like the time of year here when winter turns into spring. I sat exhausted, with a body that had long been collapsing, in a blue plastic chair near the cistern. Around me was new grass, the buzzing of bees, insects, crawling ants and the green onions my mother had planted in a primitive bed. O God! I had forgotten that in this world there were bees buzzing, ants crawling, green grass, green onions and a warm sun. And paying attention to what I had forgotten, or even betrayed, was the winning card for the will for life that was getting ready to be born in me.

Once I read a story about two sisters living in an old apartment building in some city. Above them lived an ageing painter. Every time he met one of them on the stairs, he smiled and said, 'One day I will paint my masterpiece and sell it, and will travel round the world with you.' His hair turned grey, and still he repeated the same promise. The sisters got used to him, so much so that they forgot his existence. There are those who get so used to things that they forget that things exist!

Then one of the sisters fell ill. She lay in bed near a window that looked over orchards full of bare trees. It was snowing and windy, and from one tree by the window the leaves were falling, one after the other. The sick woman was convinced that she would die when the last leaf fell from that tree. She began to fade away, and the leaves continued to fall, until 'the last leaf' remained. A day or two passed, and the leaf was still in place in spite of the wind and the snow. The sister started to regain her desire to live until, one day, she recovered her health. She then came down to look at that leaf. When she climbed the tree, she found it was painted onto one of the branches.

The painter used to light his lamp every night, climb the tree and paint a leaf that would never fall. The woman returned to her apartment. When she met the painter on the stairs, before he could utter a word, she said, 'You have painted your masterpiece.'

As for me, I felt that every leaf in the orchards, every yellow fennel blossom and every ant and bee and insect on that warm morning were my 'first leaf' and the 'masterpiece of the orchards'. My destiny is being born, and the earth is painting it.

Yes, yes. I know that my vision of the Inner Monastery and the almond orchards is like a fairy tale; for the Inner Monastery is a blessed olive tree that belongs neither to the east nor to the west, and its oil almost shines even though no fire touches it. And I and the badgers and the partridges and the gazelles and the ululating snake and Qaddura and my mother's memory are drops of that oil. This is called 'the reach of the olives in the oil'. I like this expression, 'The reach of the olive in the oil'. I heard it for the first time in Ramallah during the First Intifada in an empty street, after the funeral of a child who had been martyred. No one was about. I was on my way back home when I saw an elderly woman of the fellahin, wearing an embroidered dress that resembled a painting drawn with coloured thread and needles. It had every possible colour of every possible season. It was, I mean the surface of the dress, was like a 'leaf that never falls'. Fellahin women have dignity and pride. She reached out her hand to me because she was poor. But instead of begging, she started to sing:

> May God grant you a marble stone
> That can't be moved or removed
> By the wish of the envious, or the will of the ruler
> May God grant you the stone of the house
> And extend the reach of your life
> Like the reach of the olive in the oil

And if the olive can reach into its oil, then the Mountain can reach into its olive trees. Yes, yes. I know that my vision itself, this very vision, is another fairy tale from the tales of this mountain. I never knew Qaddura. I never saw him, and never heard his rabab. To me he is a fairy tale from tales of the Inner Monastery. And I, fascinated with him, am also a fairy tale about his fairy tale, a tale about another tale. The true teller is the Monastery. I mean, 'this mountain'—not me, not my mother, not Qaddura, and not the rabab.

I became dependent on returning to the Inner Monastery to ask its mountain about my beginnings in it. It is accurate to say that I myself am nothing more than the question of this mountain about its endings, a question that reaches into its plants, its partridges, its badgers, its gazelles, its vipers and its people. Yes, yes, I know. My way of thinking about everything is a fairy tale of the mountain, from the remainders of my beginnings in Qaddura to the remainders of my endings in the moonlit shadows of the almond trees. When as a child I read the poem by Mahmoud Darwish,

> In the rubble is our rose
> And our faces on the sand
> If the summer winds blows
> We'll unfurl our kerchiefs
> Slowly, slowly . . .

I imagined I was lying face down in the ruins of the Inner Monastery at high noon. I believe also that my own fairy tale will reach into my oil, I mean, into my young son, Áthar.

Before he was born, I didn't know what to call him. Then in a dream I saw a horizon in which were seven layers of twilight behind a mountain of thorns, the very mountains on which sits the Monastery but it was distorted in the dream. In dreams, places become the masks of the spirit. And I heard a deep melodious voice saying again and again: 'Áthar, Áthar!'

This name is an action. Yes, an action—for action is important in life. It comes from the same root that gives us 'ruins' 'traces' and 'altruism'. I called him 'Áthar' but I did not realize that with this name I was going to return to my ruins and to what I have 'preferred'. The sound that came to me in the dream was that of the Inner Monastery, or perhaps its invocation. In it there is a hidden music, perhaps the echo of Qaddura's rabab. Who knows?

I had an intuition that we, Áthar and I, knew each other in a previous life. I imagined that Áthar's spirit, and my spirit, have known each other since Canaanite times and lived among the shepherds in the 'land of the gazelle and the colour purple'. Then they wandered through time until one of them settled in my body. As for the other spirit, his spirit, it kept on living in caves and horizons, watching me, until the time for its incarnation arrived, and it cried out in the twilight, 'Call him Áthar.'

He was born during a bitter cold winter at the Red Crescent hospital in Ramallah, and there I witnessed for the first time the process of childbirth—the contractions of labour and the expansion of the womb till slowly, slowly, the head of a confused being (and confusing to another) emerges. I felt I was watching my own birth also, the birth of a being who will one day ask the Inner Monastery, 'Where did I come from? And where am I going?' And the answer will be, 'To the crescent moon over the Mountain!' I said to Áthar, 'Welcome to your first day on this earth.'

In those days, he and my wife Petra and I lived at the bottom of a hill in Birzeit in a house that looked out on a wood with pine and cypress and almond trees—the same kind of trees that my father had planted around our house in 1948. Áthar will grow up here, near the shadows of my memory, with my wife and myself as the two olive trees whose reaching oil he will be—a fairy tale about them.

From the day of his birth, above the woods there was the whirring of Israeli helicopters. He would hear that whirring sound at night, and trace its movement by moving his head under the faint light of the candle as if he were following his destiny, or as if he were a sunflower shadowing a day of resurrection. And I thought, 'He'll walk, not the road of no-return, or the road of clarity, but the path of uncertainty, like me.'

The first word he uttered was 'aeroplane'. My own first memory was the forced evacuation of my family as 'foreign nationals' by aeroplane from Beirut. I don't understand the meaning of these paradoxes which interlock my life with his. As if he were me, or I were him. It happened that one day we went with him, his mother Petra and I, to the Golan Heights, to visit a Druze saint's tomb. I asked an elder there about the meaning of 'aeroplane' being the first word he had uttered. The elder said, 'When a child speaks the first word, we, the Druze, say, "he has spoken", and thus has entered the cycle of reincarnation. An older soul settles into the new-born, and speaks its first words through him—perhaps the beginning of its own past, or the beginning of its future.'

It was not in vain that Áthar's questions were bigger than him, and too strange for a child who hadn't yet reached a year and a half to be asking, for they were the questions of the soul that spoke through him, the soul of these mountains.

Once he asked: 'Hussein, who poured the dirt over the Mountain?' I was holding him in my arms, looking out at the woods. I didn't know how to answer. So I said, 'Who but the rabbit would pour the dirt over the Mountain?' Another time he brought me a fountain pen and asked, 'Hussein, does this pen write poetry?' I answered, 'Yes.' And he asked, 'What is the colour of poetry?' 'The fountain pen with red ink writes red poetry, and the one with green ink write green poetry.' Another time, he saw an anthill in the wood and started to dance, turning round and round and singing. Then he said, 'Hussein, this is an anthill. Dance! Dance!' And I danced. It was as if I was learning to pay attention to the little details (and God is in the details!) from this Great Spirit that spoke through him.

It was absolutely certain that all of us, Petra, Áthar and I, would one day return to the Inner Monastery, not so that the fairy tale of this Mountain should reach its end but so that it would continue. And return we did. We visited the cave with the rectangular door, and told Áthar it was the cave of Aladdin. Owner of the magic lantern. He went inside and started playing, saying that Aladdin was late in returning to his cave today. At that moment, I had the overwhelming feeling that we, the three of us, were born 'outside time'.

One day, the ancient Pharaohs decided to change their lunar year from 365 days to 360. Ordinary people could not understand how five days had disappeared, and so they said that the moon goddess Isis had lost them in a game of dominoes with one of the great gods. And thus anyone who was born during these five days would be born 'outside time'. And, to a certain extent, this means that anyone born during these five days would also be born 'in lost time', or the time that is 'surplus to need'—and that means birth in a more ancient and more authentic time, one that memory has forgotten or pretends to forget. Secondly, this also means birth outside of rotating time, the perfectly circular time upon which all agree; and birth outside of this time would mean that the new-born would not be part of the area of the circle, or of any point on its circumference. They would, quite simply, be 'outside time'. Is this also a fairy tale? Yes, yes, yes.

The three of us were in the cave when I started to recall my most difficult times—when, sometime before the present Intifada, I smelt death in the air, and my face died. I do not think anyone had heard of the death of faces yet. I said to Petra that she, Áthar and I had to emigrate, perhaps to Canada, before the smell of death spread further. Escape! But Palestine is a cage. I started to have night sweats. I would wake up to the light of a faint red lamp, soaking with sweat, my shirt wet enough to wring, as if it had been dipped in a basin of water. A strange pain in the belly and the back, exhaustion, loss of appetite, loss of weight and an itch under the skin. I collapsed. The Mountain fell sick with cancer.

I started secretly to return to the moonlit mountains of childhood, to this beauty that I had once betrayed. It was not a well-planned return. I discovered that I was the child of life, not death. Something in the Mountain was saying to me: 'Even if you have only two years to live, two years here are better than two centuries there.' Resist! This land is yours. Resist! I was standing at the window, looking out on the woods—the pine and almond trees—and it occurred to me that Petra would collapse if I collapsed. 'Resist, not for your own sake. Resist!' I felt that the Mountain was crying out to me: 'Say to her, "Whatever happens, when you visit me, I will be among the almond trees. It will be sunny, and light will diffuse in the air. There will be orchards, bees, and the path of bees", and until that time comes, resist!'

At first the haematologist said I might have AIDS. O God! We're finished, all of us! Petra, Áthar and I. It doesn't matter about me. My disease is a game between God and me. But what about them? Áthar would run towards me, laughing and turning his head left and right. He'd laugh: 'Oh! Oh! Hussein, Hussein, look!' And I would try to imagine that he was going to die in a year, or five years, from AIDS, and then my imagination would come to a halt. I had not said anything to Petra yet. I thought it would be preferable to go to the sea and commit suicide by drowning. Yet the sea returns bodies to the shore, and they will find me. I don't have the right to be a coward, to escape in this manner. I was thinking of Petra and Áthar, not of myself. We had been at the

Canabata Café. I placed my hand on her shoulders, and said, 'If I'm infected with AIDS, then you are too.' 'It doesn't matter. What does matter is that we'll die together.' Petra is great, a great woman. Will she be able to take the second shock? 'And Áthar will also be infected' 'Áthar, no! Áthar, no, no! It doesn't matter about me, but Áthar, no!'

At the Ramallah hospital there was a nurse with a hijab and a supernatural face—ecclesiastical, neutral, severe. She drew my blood for a test. A face that cannot be forgotten, ever. In one week, these two stern lips will open and utter my fate—'negative' or 'positive'. One word could condemn us all to death, or allow us to live. Let it be capital punishment, then, if it has to be! Yet I didn't want to hear this word from this nurse in particular. Her face was one of the signs of the Resurrection, or that's how it seemed to me. On the wall, in front of the blood bank, was a board on which was written: 'Cancer cures one from smoking!' Cancer is a rose, a grace from God. My wish now is to have the disease of cancer, rather than AIDS. Yet the sign betrays a lack of sensitivity towards those who do have cancer. The language of the healthy and that of the sick are two different languages with a barrier between them.

A week passed that resembled Rimbaud's *A Season in Hell*. I returned to the laboratory through a set of glass doors to find another nurse with a set of papers in her hands. 'I'm Hussein. I want the result of the test for AIDS.' As she searched through the papers, I was in another world. Under my name was the word 'negative', which meant that I didn't have AIDS. I said to her, 'Negative. That means I'm not infected. No AIDS. 'Yes. Negative means negative. That means you're not infected.' 'True?' 'True. That means I'm not infected.' This was too much for her, but I carried on, 'Negative means I'm not infected.' She laughed and shook her head.

I had imagined that I would start dancing or crying if I was not infected. But what took place was not this or that. I found myself turning my head to the left and to the right, and running down the corridors of the hospital, shouting, 'Oh! Oh! Hussein, Hussein! Look!' I was repeating Áthar's word. I had become Áthar. I was no longer me, I had returned to childhood. The haematologist stopped me in the hallway. Surrounded by other patients, I said, 'Negative. That means I'm not infected with AIDS.'

And he said, 'The lab report arrived. You have lymphoma.' But that was not important now, because Petra and Áthar were outside this game which I can play on my own with destiny.

I came running out of the hospital, not laughing or crying. And all of a sudden I leant my head against the trunk of a pine tree in the street and burst into old and bitter tears. My body had been rigid to the point of dullness, and now it melted in a fit of crying. I did not cry, not once, inside that hell, but the moment I walked out of it I cried. It was now my turn to be concerned, not with Petra or with Áthar, but with my own self and their survival.

We emerged from the cave, and suddenly Áthar reached out his empty hand to me and said, 'Hussein, take Aladdin and put him in your pocket. It's cold outside.' I put Aladdin in my pocket, and he raised Aladdin's magic lantern with his other hand. Perhaps he imagined the lantern to be made of a pure gold that was green in colour, and shining in the night like a pearl in the middle of a rose garden. When we reached the house, he asked, 'Hussein, is Aladdin in your pocket.' 'Yes.' 'Is he warm enough?' 'Yes. Yes.'

Two days later, while I was about to set out for the Inner Monastery, after we had moved to the countryside near Ramallah, my brother Fadi said, 'One of the fellahin was at the Inner Monastery yesterday, and he almost died.' 'Almost died?' 'Yes. He ran into five armed settlers and started shaking with fear. But they were merry, carrying narghiles as though they were Arabs, and asked him where was the most beautiful spot for smoking.' 'And then?' He said, "Here. Here is the most beautiful spot." '

Oh, God! I thought about the story. They were not just settlers but also belonged to special assassination squads, the 'Arabizers'. They dress like Arabs, smoke narghile like Arabs and their mission is to liquidate activists in the Intifada. Perhaps they had observed my moonlit visits to the monastery; or seen Áthar as he was carrying Aladdin's lamp; or Petra, who in any case is a refugee from pre-1948 Palestine and who saw in the Inner Monastery what she had never dreamt of—land. And they had now come to liquidate us.

I gathered a group of my friends, a woman who had returned from Tunisia, the poet Kifah Fanni, Áthar, Petra and myself (yes, I'm one of my friends) and went to the Monastery. We lit a fire, and sat around it. From a small settlement near that of Halamish came—interrupted by the whirring of military helicopters—loud and agitated music in Hebrew, its Western sound mixed with the sounds of the East. 'Soon, on a moonlit, spacious and very quiet night,' I thought, 'the Arabizers will come here and sit among the ruins of the Monastery above the sound of Qaddura's rabab, and smoke their narghiles. Maybe they too will have their own rabab and play it to the sound of their own laughter. I will pass from far away, very far away, on the other side of the moonlit meadow, and in complete secrecy I will sneeze faint sneezes like the gazelles, and no one other than me will remember Qaddura's rabab here, or Snuffie, or the sound that cried like a little child or know that the viper that trills will not come.'

Who knows? Maybe the Arabizers will hear the sound of the ghreriya itself, the sound that resembles the crying of a small child, and chase it about the moonlit orchards. The sound will seem to be coming from the first field, but when they reach it, it will seem to be coming from the second, or from no-place, and they will certainly say that these are crazy mountains, inhabited by other myths than their myths, and other tales than their tales. Or, more simply, inhabited by goyim [aghyār], beings who are not of their kind. And perhaps I will be this ghreriya, but certainly not the last ghreriya in these mountains.

I asked my mother, 'Do you know the ghreriya?' She answered, 'Its size is approximately that of a cat. And it does not have an elongated body but one that is more circular.' That will be my shape, and I will live in the dreams of this mountain. It will dream of me, and I will dream of it. But what will the ghreriya's dream of the Mountain be like? And what will the Mountain's dream of it be like? These are questions with no answers. But no one, not even an exorcist, can bring me out of the dream of the Mountain, or its dream of me.

CHAPTER TWO

LAND OF TALES

Whenever I walk among the ruins of the Inner Monastery by the light of a full moon, I realize how far away it sits in the wilds. No one would live here except for a wild animal or a god (to quote Aristotle). It has the majesty of antiquity. In my imagination, I see it rising anew from its ruins, illuminated by the light of a lamp made of clay, its wick immersed in olive oil. The lamp would be in a courtyard paved with small, polished mosaic tiles, from where would well up, under the faint light of the stars, the footsteps of the monks and their chants from an age when the stars were signs of destiny. Around it, outside the walls, would be foxes, hyenas, the jinn and a plenitude of invisible beings. A place that is totally 'outer', yet my ancestors called it 'the inner', as though it were closer than their jugulars; for the name itself is magical to one who thinks about it, resembling a temple at the top of a mountain in the valleys of their own spirit. The outmost location and the inmost monastery—all in one name. Magic!

A Buddhist sage might say to someone who thinks like me, 'You don't see a moonlit monastery or the ruins of a monastery. Rather, your mind flows outside itself. Then it freezes, taking the shape of what appears in your eyes to be a moonlit monastery and the ruins of a monastery. You mind is seeing itself, and nothing more.' So be it! In the outmost part of my soul is an 'inner monastery', and the story of Qaddura is its gate.

And Qaddura was here 'before the trees were tall'. I can still hear him playing his rabab from the roof of the Monastery as though he has not stopped being a highwayman even after his death. And he brings my memory to a standstill next to him with a single vibrating string and a song, so that my beginnings will be as a highwayman and nothing else. He was a blond man with blue eyes, living at the Monastery with Kayid, the most powerful among his brothers and his right arm. They married the same woman, Snuffie, and had only one child by her.

Kayid married Snuffie first, and she gave birth to several children who all died one after the other. She smelt the smell of death in her womb, a ruin of some sort. And when God finally granted her a son, Nayef, perhaps because of her feeling of ruin, she started roaming around the ancient caves close to the Monastery, in which large skeletons lay in a basin from the time of the Romans, or even the Canaanites. Wanting to remove the smell of death from the place, she scooped out the bones, swept away the dirt and then returned to the Monastery, exhausted. She dressed Nayef in his best and most beautiful clothes, perfumed his body and fell asleep on the mat close by him. Then she had a very strange dream indeed.

She dreamt that the monastery was empty, and lit with lanterns. Its gates were open, through which a woman entered, dressed in black. Silent, she stood among the shadows at the furthest corner, as if she were a guardian or an ancient priestess. She gazed at Snuffie for a while, and then said, 'You removed the bones of our dead, and now you lie here at rest? I will bring Nayef out of *his* monastery!'

Snuffie woke up from her dream in a fright. She rubbed her eyes, but saw no one. She then uttered the formula for seeking refuge in God, and looked at Nayef. She shook him, but he did not move. The silence of death was in him; his body was lifeless. My mother said that Snuffie took an oath that evening that never, ever, as long as she lived, would she touch any bones from times past. And perhaps this is what made her become midwife to the village towards the end of her life. She chose to bring birth to the future rather than remove the bones of the past.

It was the custom of the women of our tribe in those days to celebrate the 'Thursday of the Dead.' A Thursday with pagan roots, one of the most ancient rites of spring and rebirth. They used to boil a great number of eggs along with onion skins. The eggs would turn red-brown, dyed with the colours of the earth. They also baked leavened bread, turned yellow like lemons from the granules of turmeric sprinkled into the dough, and then they carried what they had baked and boiled on trays made of straw that had also been dyed and woven into colourful geometric patterns that were part of the ancient customs of this region. Carrying these colours of resurrection on a warm Thursday in spring, when the smooth, blue flowers of the basalon shrub dotted the ground, they visited the graveyard and sat among the shrubs by the graves of loved ones. They divided the eggs and sweets and bread among the children in the hope that their dead would rise on the day of Resurrection like the grass that split open the earth's crust in order to grow; or like the hatching chicks that cut through the eggshell in order to be born; or like the colours themselves that were resurrected in spring. These were women's rites in which no men took part.

But on these occasions Snuffie did not carry her tray to the common graveyard. She took the sweets and bread and eggs to a cave called al-Murabbiya where they had buried Nayef. She sat in the humidity, in the particular smell of a cave that resembles a pistachio closed in on itself but that has opened only to allow a dead child in. She cried, as though the tears were rain to which she was appealing for help to bring Nayef back to life together with the narcissus flowers, the chrysanthemums, the greenness of grass and the sun. When night fell she would still be sitting by her tray. Once, she suddenly heard sounds from the depths of the cave, the sounds of an obscure collapse, as though one side of the Mountain was going to crumble. Then she heard the neighing of a horse that was more akin to the neighing of the jinn. She was so terrified she could not stand up. Shaking in fear, and creeping backwards on her haunches until she reached the entrance, she left her tray behind and escaped by the skin of her teeth.

When Qaddura heard about Nayef and Snuffie's dream, he did not say a word. Even after some time had passed, he remained silent. He was harder than a stone, yet more sensitive than the string of his rabab. He did not say what was in his heart except to his rabab. He used to smoke the narghile on the roof of the Monastery, and contemplate the moonlit wadis all around him. My mother spent the evenings with him, along with Snuffie and his sister. He took his rabab and started singing about the white nights that never came to erase the blackness of the dark nights, and about the promises of lucky stars that never arrived except to pass like an evanescent fancy. Then he sang about 'the stranger of the Mountain'—referring to the one who did not understand the logic of the place for which she had left her village, and remained a stranger in it. Snuffie was from another branch of our tribe, from a different village—hence, she was a 'stranger' (she was not 'from here'). She caught the hint about *here*, but I do not know how she felt about what he had sung.

My mother was a 'stranger' too, and knew very well the feelings of female strangers. For she had been brought up as an orphan, and then became a dancer and singer at the festivals of the fellahin. I asked her about the feeling of the female strangers who were like Snuffie, and she sang:

O riders on horses, visit for me the one you love
And if your horses fall short
Keep your own strong resolve!

I then saw Snuffie as she sat on the roof of the Monastery, with Qaddura singing, gazing at the moonlit mountains far away to the North and imagining that her family had come, riding on seven white horses, over paths through the desolate mountains, to visit her—the stranger. Perhaps none of them ever came, not even on feast days, and she was sad because she was the 'stranger to the Mountain'.

Don't go up the ladder
The West wind is blowing
What burns the heart
More than night and exile?

In spite of her life of exile, Snuffie's spirit did not break, nor the spirit of my mother, at the Inner Monastery for as long as Qaddura was alive. So much so that his sister was touched by rapture one morning, and slipped away into the orchards, in a dancing fit, all on her own. She sang and laughed among the olive trees, until they thought she had lost her sanity. And when they stopped her, she said, 'How can a woman not dance with men like this around her?' She was referring to Qaddura and his brother, and carried on with her dancing.

Kayid died suddenly. A preordained death. Qaddura married his widow Snuffie and adopted her daughter Nayfa. Nayfa was a mere child who knew nothing about the world, and was given in marriage to another child, even younger, from a village near Nablus—a far-away place in the wilds, in those days. She used to take off the white hat from her 'bridegroom's' head, and then the two of them would play with it in the dirt.

One day, in the mountains, Nayfa's mother-in-law bit her on the shoulder because she had gathered more wood than she had. Unable to bear that insult, Nayfa waited till early morning, then sneaked out of her room, opened the door of the house and headed out on foot for the Inner Monastery, back to her origin and beginnings in that Mountain. The road was desolate, populated only by ghouls, hyenas, jinn and other beings. When evening came, she saw lanterns in the house of one of the fellahin. She knocked on his door, and slept there for the night.

When her in-laws woke up and could not find her, they sent a rider to the Inner Monastery to bring her back. He arrived before Nayfa did. Qaddura took his shotgun, mounted his horse and went searching for her in the mountains. Finally, he found her at the bottom of a ravine, and sat her on the horse behind him. When he brought her back to the Monastery, he said to the rider, 'She won't return until you pay the price of her getting lost in the mountains.' 'And what would that be?' 'You took from her a gold medallion attached to a chain of gold. Give her back her medallion.' These medallions were rare, and the rider searched a long time until he found an Ottoman medallion with an elderly woman in one of the villages. He bought it, and brought it back to the monastery. Qaddura turned the medallion over in his hands, and said, 'She won't return until you pay her full dowry.' 'But we've already paid it.' 'Pay it a second time. That's the price of her dignity.'

A year passed before the family were able to raise the new dowry, and when they brought it to the Monastery, Qaddura said, 'She came to the Monastery on the run, and she won't leave except as a new bride. You must celebrate her wedding again.' After they had celebrated her wedding again, he stopped them at the door, and said, 'Before you take her away, I have another condition: if she comes back humiliated another time, you'll have to pay the price of Qaddura's dignity, which is very expensive. You won't be able to afford it.'

No wonder his sister went dancing in the orchards until they thought she had lost her mind 'because she had brothers like these'!

As for why I am now recalling these tales of the Mountain while walking, as always, among the moonlit almond orchards around our house, barely breathing and facing the spectre of death because of a new swelling in the my lungs—that is another matter. Perhaps with these tales I can breathe the air of other places and other times in order to sense another moonlit space inside my being and return to whatever inner monastery there was in my spirit that would grant me the strength of beginnings so as to face the cruelty of endings. For imagination is power.

Yet the swelling intensified. I was no longer able to breathe— my chest was closing in on itself. The haematologist said that morning, 'The cancer may have returned.' He was nervous because Áthar was with me. 'Why do you bring your children to hospitals? There are germs and diseases here. Take him home, and then come back! Your condition is critical.' Nothing ever ends completely in this Holy Land; everything returns, as al-Mutanabbi says:

That which already passed keeps coming back
Because what will come has already passed

I spent seventeen days at the Ramallah hospital in a room that opened out onto a corridor whose fluorescent lights were always turned on. Natural light had not entered the place for decades, and it never will. It seems as though one of the basics of hospital and prison architecture in our lands is to subject patients and prisoners to isolation by light, for hospital and prison are two sides of a single comparison.

When the Palestinian Authority took over the Ramallah prison from the Israeli Occupation forces, they opened it to ordinary visitors and those previously held in it, and there I saw the art of architectural design stripped of all pretensions. A cell that I could not reach, even at the height of noon, except through a dark tunnel leading to a cave, forcing me to light matches in order to see in the darkness. I found myself at the head of stairs made of stone. To the left was a metal handrail, and to the right a humid wall that appeared to have been constructed with special care. Beyond the last step was a rectangular pool, and, immediately to the left of the handrail, another pool. Both pools held water to the depth of at least one metre. Brackish water turning green, with straw and insects floating on top, and the promise of eternal torment. Here, in the water, they used to soak the prisoner in solitary confinement. Next to me stood Jamil Abu Saada—professor of biology at Birzeit University—whose face twisted out of shape as he gazed into the water. He said, 'Hussein, here, I spent whole nights, in this very water. I couldn't sit down or stand up.'

At the end of night, when the nurses have gone to sleep and there is silence, I lean against the bedpost under the buzzing of the fluorescent lights, my entire body exhausted, perforated with needles, green and blue spots on my arms, and, in my blood, litres of medicine instead of desires—enough for me to know the meaning of 'shower of chemicals'. This is the exact expression that came to mind when they told me I would have to have chemotherapy two years ago: 'a shower of chemicals'. I had imagined that they would make me stand in a locked bathroom on a floor made of reinforced concrete (this fearful Roman invention—reinforced concrete!), and from openings in the ceiling chemical solutions would rain all over me. One of them would be a blood-red solution in a plastic bag that triggers nausea. Later, they will pour litres of it into my blood.

The room had a wide window that looked out on a deserted, still-unfinished cement hall in which empty boxes of medicines lay scattered—'gifts' from 'brothers' and 'enemies' and 'friendly enemies' to the 'people of the Intifada'. There were used needles and blood bags. Rubble all around me instead of almond orchards! I became aware of a black cat standing in the middle of the room under the ghost of a light, emaciated—in reality, a rack of bones—and sneezing violently. She shook from head to tail as she tried to expel what was in her stomach, but in vain. It seems she had swallowed some medicines, or fragments of needles, with the leftovers from the hospital food. A yellow foam came out of her mouth, and I felt that she was exactly like me, for I too wanted to remove the needles from the back of my hand, heave out all that was in my stomach and mind and leave for the Inner Monastery and the almond orchards. My mind felt like this hall, and it needed wide, moonlit spaces, open to the Milky Way and to divine architecture itself. 'How cramped life would be, except for the space that hope provides'. If only they had sedated me, instead of all this wakefulness!

I am thinking of my son Áthar. He is three now. Is he sleeping, or playing in the almond orchards and asking his mother about me? I can almost hear the sound of their laughter there, where I cannot reach, in orchards not within my grasp. I will be going back to the orchards! I will, for my body is not exactly me, regardless how far astray into it the needles may go: 'It's as if I had died before now / I know this vision . . .'

Áthar came with Petra during the morning visiting hours. I had a glimpse of him laughing as he walked in front of her in the hallway. In his small hand was an almond shoot with some tender green almonds on it. He was happy, and ran towards me: 'Hussein, Hussein! Where have you been? By Allah I've been looking for you?' And he gave me the shoot. I felt like someone standing on a foggy seashore; I could not see anything, or know exactly where I was. Then I saw him walk on the sand, through the fog—his hair washed by the roar of the sea—and he gave me a golden shoot from which a young jinni emerged to show me the way. I felt I was in a dream sent by the Mountain of the Gods—a dream that resembled the poet Mudhaffar al-Nawwab's response when they said to him, 'The sea won't take you to Basra', and he answered, 'The sea will take me to Basra, or Basra will come in a dream and take me.' The golden shoot was Basra in the dream, coming to take me outside, to a place that was no longer possible to attain, no longer within reach. Lines from Mahmoud Darwish came to mind:

> Should the tips of your hair
> Wet with sand, caress my face
> I'll end my game, I'll end it
> And head for the old house
> In the footsteps of my family
> And cry out: O stones of the house, pray!

And I did go to our old house, but in the wrong light and on a miserable evening during the Khamsin winds. How surprising to find that the green grass had turned into hopeless dry straw. Even the green almonds at the top of the trees were hard and dirty with dust. The anthills were deserted, and chaos was everywhere I looked, inside my heart and outside:

O time
Like grass spreading on walls!

I returned not because I had been cured but to travel in two days to Al-Amal Center, in Amman. Chaos in my heart, and chaos outside! But in fact there is no chaos, only another order of things perhaps.

* * *

'This evening is like the Resurrection,' I thought. I was sitting under the window of our old house before my trip when an idiotic child I knew started playing on his harmonica a tune that was distant, disturbed and lost in the air, there behind the almond orchards. And it may have been due to this playing, this particular performance, that the dust—which resembled a white smoke blown over mountains and trees by a suffocating Khamsin easterly—began to rise and gather overhead, turning into a deep yellow, a colour like pulverized gold. Then, from the west a strange redness erupted, like a flood of twilight anxiously creeping eastward, inside of which were black, green and brown whirlpools churning as if the sky itself were going to boil—and with no sun in sight, no sun at all.

To the west, in an isolated corner, a pale bluish moon appeared over the wadis, then disappeared. Suddenly over the old village the light of the full moon—bright like a moment of enlightenment—flared up from below, perhaps from the low-lying wadis, and spread as if an invisible hand were painting the horizon, depicting a moment of Sufi Illumination. The green dome of the mosque appeared as an echo of the red dome of the sky above it, and I felt that something was going to fall, that perhaps the sky itself was going to fall. A film of the strangest possible lines and colours.

As for the light, it became darker, turning translucent, then heavy over the orchards, like the shadow of a pagan god passing overhead. The wind turned into a cold westerly that almost uprooted the roses in front of me. The fragrance of wild mint and roses surged over me, yet I felt that this fragrance was a forewarning of the Resurrection, or 'is it the storm in which vision and the spirit dissolve, and the country itself dissolves?' Even my mother commented on the strangeness of the weather. She turned her eyes to the beds she had planted, and said, 'All the cats disappeared today. Not a single cat has remained here.' Behind her, over the old cistern, on the clothesline, perched a grey bird whose wings were almost torn apart by the wind, but it clung to its place tenaciously.

Áthar also, three years old now, was sitting next to me full of fear. 'Hussein,' he said, 'look at the sea above' (his name for the sky), but I did not respond. I was baffled, engrossed in watching. Then he said, 'Hussein, I want a dress.' I said, 'Dresses are for girls, and you're a boy.' 'Fine. I want to become a girl.' For a few moments I was captivated by his desire to switch. I thought: he'll be a female for seven years, like Tiresias, the Oracle of Delphi, then go back to being a male, and the almond orchards will acknowledge him as the oracle for their temple. Wise is he who speaks in the name of the gods!

Then a pomegranate tree, exceptionally green, to which I had paid no attention, claimed my attention. My mother had planted it in a primitive stone basin with straw underneath. The faint light had intensified its greenness, and its blossoms stood out—these red flowers that resemble diaphanous flames, most delicate and inspiring, like a painter's wild brush strokes on a dark green background. They radiated a luminous and strange light that could not be apprehended by reason or by revelation, like the ecstasies of the Sufis. I myself seemed more like a rumour in the ear of the place than a solid being. The world has awakened. Don't go to sleep yourself!

For some time since adulthood I had been dreaming about becoming a child again so that I could wake up. Suddenly, Áthar, as though capturing this wish from my depths, said, 'Hussein, why don't you become Áthar and I become Hussein?' Strange! My soul and his recognize each other from a previous life. Definitely; otherwise he would not have caught what I was thinking. Yes, yes, I thought. The cats have not returned and the light is strange. I'm afraid and need to escape just like the cats. 'The world is turned upside down. This rain should've come twenty days go, not now,' said my mother. 'Yes, yes. The world's turned upside down. That's certain,' I muttered in a quandary. The bird flew from the clothesline to the pomegranate tree, and paused for a moment among the lanterns of pomegranate blossoms, but could not hold its own against the gale wind. It flew at an angle, as if the wind had gulped it, somewhat as in Feiruz's song, 'And our strange story—the wind ripped it apart.'

And that idiotic boy was still playing his harmonica. Then some fragrances that I had smelt in the past, the scent of mint and comparisons buried in the soil of memory came back to life. Everything seemed like Snuffie's tray on which she had carried an entire resurrection of colours to the Cave of the Murabbiya so that she could behold the return of Nayef. The words forgotten since my previous life awakened in the eternal cycle of reincarnation, thanks to which everything returns but does not return exactly the same.

Thirty years ago, I read Darwish's line 'I imagined I was a butterfly in pomegranate blossoms'. Now I remembered the comparison as I gazed into the glowing blossoms of the pomegranate tree, but did not feel I was a white butterfly among those lanterns. I felt sick and heavy, and the furthest that one could be from the whiteness of the butterfly. Yet the lanterns were glowing in that dark light. They glowed, and nothing else did, giving off a light like a formation of candles in the hands of knights riding their horses at night in a silent wedding procession, as in the stories narrated by my family.

Is it not time for my resurrection yet? I will ripen shortly with the almonds and pomegranates and roses, and I will say to these orchards, 'I have ripened.' And if I were to laugh, the sun would shine; and if I were to cry, the rain would fall. And I will go back to being a child again. And if I cannot do this now, in this life, I will live long enough in order to find out. But in the cycle of reincarnation, in my future life, I will return to the earth and walk upon it as a child-prophet.

* * *

I travelled to the Amal Center for cancerous tumours in Amman, and stayed a whole month in Rusaifa—a city made of dust. The wait was terrifying, the wait for the test results. My body was starting to become rigid, its movements more restricted. No crying, and no happiness; a project for a statue. And whoever, like me, has transferred from one hospital to another to wait for his destiny, all chemistry of the spirit within him will rely on the force with the strongest magnetic pull in his heart. Hope; or this movie of ruin. The question I have is not when or how I am going to die, nor even about the duality of hope and ruin, but what am I going to make of myself now—how to make my end a sublime celebration of my beginnings. But, instead of the sublime celebration of my beginnings, I find myself in an American movie whose producer has AIDS, a film all in blue, in which nothing moves except the shadows of blue things, and the voice of the American producer saying, 'What kind of hell is the waiting room?' And what kind of hell is Rusaifa? A city of Khamsin dust, and a desert noon that feels like a 'reality fried to 45 degrees Centigrade'.

A horizon made of mountains of sand whose colour has been extinguished, and houses made of reinforced concrete, grey and heavier than the weather itself, seeming to be an architectural dissonance or a miscarriage. Not one flower. Very sparse vegetation, visual deprivation and spaces that produce a hunger for colour. And to counter the power of this place to bore the eyes, they celebrated it with every possible synthetic and garish colour. In every house I entered, there were substitutes for the deadness of the desert and the architecture.

For example, I stayed for a time in a 'villa' with a large living room whose furniture was all gilded, radiating at night a colour as yellow as gold veins in the rock. On the walls were gilded boards in the shape of closed doors, no less garish, on which were carved verses from the Qur'an. In the corners artificial flowers of red cloth or green plastic branched out. In another living room, scattered around a colour television, were end tables with mirrored tops that reflected everything set upon them; and near the television, to the right, was a fish tank, also coloured, in which little waterfalls were lit with a blue light from a glass bottom that resembled the ocean. Everything was kitsch—bright, shiny and pointing to a bad taste that was not conscious of being so.

The secret of all this kitsch lay in the inhabitants' efforts to make the inside of the house a world of its own—an oasis, even if banal, a Thursday of the Dead of a different sort—and a refuge from the deadness of colourless nature outside.

Rusaifa is nothing but a shopping centre, with shops and pharmacies and restaurants and stores selling cloth and electrical appliances—for example—but not a single cafe worth sitting in; no place for escaping the dust or dearth of colour, and no spectacle other than the signboard displays in clashing colours. Merely living here is a misunderstanding with God. I was overwhelmed by a feeling of being in chains, without any alternatives: from a humane perspective, it was not possible for me to remain yet it was also not possible for me to leave. I could be anything I wanted to be here, except myself.

I escape to the house, and sit for hours, even days, without movement, gazing at a point in front of me on the floor, or sleeping. Meanwhile, my body is becoming more rigid, and I dream of being a sculptor so that I can carve this hardening of my body in stone. No wonder that people who live here are afflicted by an abnormal religious anxiety. Here the world is suspect, and anything that connects to any real world is but a mere illusion.

* * *

Paul Klee once said that the painter does not paint the visible: he makes it visible. Cancer is a painter that made visible what I could not see with my eyes, with the coming together of the spirit of art, love and death.

From the very beginning, for example, after my first chemotherapy session, I could not walk the corridor of the Beit Jala hospital without feeling that reaching its end was going to be impossible. It seems that distance increases when we are not able to walk. Sometimes my eyes would not be able to focus, and I would see nothing except a white light like a glistening drizzle. I could not perceive anything with it, or through it, and I would almost stumble. I would have to rest after every step, and the details would loom larger and stand out. All my attention would focus on a spot of dust on a neglected corner of the dresser that no one had bothered to clean, or a piece of paper that had been thrown away, or a black insect on the window, beating its wings in the sun but not flying away. It was as if another universe that I had not noticed before, or had forgotten, was suddenly making itself present to my awareness.

At night a silver-coloured spot on the door handle shines brightly under the fluorescent light, or on the edge of a glass of orange juice. I lose myself in the light. Not only are things alienated from my eyes, my eyes are also alienated from things. A visitor accompanying one of the patients passes in front of the door. He sees an orange in front of me and quickly turns his gaze away, for this is an orange for the sick and may infect him. It radiates the energy of sickness, waking his fear that the same thing that happened to me might happen to him.

There were visitors who felt pity for me, and others who were terrified. Others yet subsisted on the fears of the sick, like the man from the Daʿwa movement: sirwāl, beard, sandals and a strange appearance, as if he were one of the People of the Cave. He took one look at my wife and was sexually aroused. He started toing and froing, and every time he passed by the door, he greeted us and then came in 'to show right guidance to his brother in Islam', but his eyes would be staring at my wife, and he did not see that I saw. Feeling that I had become 'another kind' of human being, alienated, I gazed at the glow of the orange and said nothing to him:

The orange illuminates our estrangement
The orange illuminates
The jasmine inflames our isolation
And the jasmine is innocent.

Details, details, details. As though every soap bubble has become a universe. I stay up, gazing at the door that opens onto an empty corridor with faint red lighting on the second floor. An old man from the south, wearing a black aba and a large sirwāl, looks in. With a tattoo on his chin, a thick headband and a scruffy keffiyeh, he looks as though he has jumped out of a film on primitive art. In his hand is a glass of camel milk. I have seen him earlier that day in the afternoon, when he stood at the door and said that the best treatment for cancer was camel milk from Sinai. 'And how am I to get hold of camel milk from Sinai? I hardly ever run into a camel more than once in a half a century.'

'Camel milk is a soap bubble,' said the tumour specialist, and laughed. 'Not all the camel milk in the Empty Quarter will be of any use.' Yes! But the will searches for a solution, even if it is a bubble. 'How cramped life would be, except for the space that hope provides,' even for a while.

And now he had come with a bottle of camel milk from Tuqūʿ. I was surprised by the generosity of his spirit. What am I to him that he should bring me camel milk from the south, and how did he come by it? I drank a sour hope, white, and at once heaved out all that was in my stomach.

When I fell ill, I thought I would die in a year, or two. There would be no home for my wife and my son after I was gone. I started dreaming of building a home for them in the countryside, with red soil around it, a fence made of dry wood and a small garden. I would plant onions, garlic, mint, tomatoes and a lemon tree. And in spring, on a cold morning, I would pick onions and garlic and mint and a lemon, and with my own hands I would make a salad for Áthar and Petra. I would make it myself—that was a condition. The whole idea lay at the heart of it all. Then I would wake Áthar and his mother, and we would sit at a primitive wooden table, or in the shadow of an olive tree, and eat it together. This would be my celebration of life: a bowl of salad.

> The first time they brought me into the prison yard
> And I leaned on the wall in the sun,
> I was full of wonder that the sky was so blue
> And so far away from me

Thus said Nazim Hikmet. The secret is in the details. Details now, not what passed or will come, but a bowl of salad, a pause under a sky so blue, a cat licking its paws near me and Áthar playing in the dirt. That is all I want. Have my dreams also shrunk to this extent?

Cancer is an artist that makes the little details visible, and life itself into an art. And what would it be, if it were not art?

* * *

After a month of testing, the cancerous tumour specialist at the Al-Amal Center said, 'We're done with testing. Good news! The cancer hasn't returned. You're well. But there's swelling with an area of 22 square centimetres in the lobe of your left lung. We'll treat it with cortisone. No need for the hospital. You can now go back to—', but before he had finished, I said, 'To the almond orchards.'

He wrote out the prescription for the drug. I smiled, and thought, 'The cancer has not returned because now I'm not I. I've gone back to being a child, and the cancer has struck a desperate person of very advanced age inside me. Another person who is not like me at all.'

I left the Center smiling, and the first thing I did was to stand in the shade among the pine trees near the University of Jordan hospital, and as the holy sages of the East said, 'If you stand in the right place within yourself, then where you are standing is the right place.'

I have been wanting to travel for a long time. On the back of a camel, for instance, or in a car or a boat, in order to see many places where my memory will be clear of hospital labyrinths and my nose free of the smell of drugs.

Two days later, I find myself walking at night by the shore of the Red Sea with Áthar, Petra and a friend who had invited us there. The foam gleams silver. The sea is dark, rumbling from beneath the waves, from right and left and from far and near. And I walk and walk, the sound washing my memory. No labyrinths leading to operating rooms, no needles, no hospitals, no camel milk, no smell of medicine—to forget, that is what I want, to forget. The sea washes my mind, though all this rumbling and foaming is barely enough, just barely. I walk silently, the cool air branching deep into my lungs. My feet are bare in the sand, and I walk, forever. I want nothing else but this moment. I have time only to feel the sound of the waves washing the very bottom of my brain. There is nothing else besides this sound.

The next day, the same friend invited us to visit the city of Petra. Petra is amazing. I had been dreaming of it for decades. My wife's original name was Eiman, but I gave her the name, 'Petra, the Rose City'.

It was a special treat for me that Petra should now be entering the city of her name. She seemed almost a queen on a chariot pulled by the horses of ancient Nabateans. And I, who am I? I am the riotous charioteer who is chuckling because he has not lost the game yet. If fire worshippers dreamt of movement and energy, the sculptors of this city carved their will into the rock in worship of permanence and beauty, like their brothers, the builders of the Pyramids who discovered the art of embalming mummies. Between fire and a Petra, or between fire and a mummy, the spirit moves in us all. If we lean towards fire, all permanence becomes an illusion; and if we lean towards Petra, all movement becomes an illusion. All visual art, for example, alternates between the movement of fire and the permanence of the Pyramids, or Petra. And what is the fear of death if it were not also the fear of transformation, that is, the anxiety of fire in all us.

Petra in the city of her name!

As for my name, Hussein, there is no city named Hussein. I have always felt I had no connection with it at all. There is no city for me. My relationship with it resembled Chekov's story, 'My Name and Me'. What is amusing is the family name itself, 'Barghouthi' ('Flea-like'). What horizon does a name like that create? What city can we find named after a flea? When we were married, Petra asked me, 'Why did they call you Barghouthis?' and I laughed back, 'In reference to lions.'

As for the name of my father, Jamil ('handsome'), it is a beautiful name, but common to the point of boredom. A name is like a city; each has its dwellers, suggesting something shared between those who have the same name—more so than in a real city. My name is entirely wrong. It is not so surprising that I would not know what to name my son, Áthar, before he was born.

I had thought of naming him Lorca. 'No! No!' said the painter Ibrahim Al Muzain. 'The name Lorca will dominate him all his life, and bring him to Spain.' Why not?

I also thought of naming him Al-Mu'tamid, after Al-Mu'tamid Ibn Abbad, the Andalusian poet-prince who married an eccentric woman. One day she stood by the window of the palace and said she loved the sight of snow in the mountains in spring, over there! And he planted the mountains with almond trees for her, so that their blossoms would appear like snow in spring.

Al-Mu'tamid has his own story. Once his daughters asked him to let them walk barefoot in the mud like the fellahin, and he mixed musk and camphor for them on the floor of the palace hall so that they could do so. After he lost his kingdom, he ended up in prison in Aghmat, lamenting that his daughters were

Stepping in the mud, their feet bare
As if they had never walked on musk and camphor.

The poet then starts to reproach life:

Who, after you, lives a kingship that makes him happy
Is living only the delusion of his dreams.

I do not want the name of my son's city to be the city of lost desires, and defeated princes, like Al-Mu'tamid. I was baffled, until a voice came to me from the unknown in a dream, calling out to me that his name was Áthar, Áthar, Áthar! That is, it was not I who gave him his name, and I therefore do not know the city of his name. No one else has a name like this, and there is no obscure city of the name such as this one, known only to God. Perhaps that was what drove me to read Italo Calvino's *Invisible Cities*.

I had imagined that I would go to the Inner Monastery, searching for 'a city for my name' that I could call 'Qaddura'— Qaddura's city. It would be one of the invisible cities, and its streets would be made of tales. I would build it with my voice, and the voice of my mother, and transfer it to any lips that tell stories. A city made of dust:

Where are you from?

I'm from the country of tales.

Among my friends would be Ali Baba and Enkidu, and all those who were born, who loved and lived in stories. Stories are the windows of the spirit and the imagination. When, for example, Qaddura spread his aba on the roof of the monastery and sang and played his rabab, looking out on moonlit wadis, on orchards ploughed and planted, on wide and obscure distances, he opened a window for his voice in the moonlit space and his voice occupied an eternal domain. His song would then become the city of his name:

Where are you from?

I'm from the country of windows.

If the Inner Monastery is the city of my name, or, let us say, its symbol, then it is a city that flies as the colourful rogue snake flew over the moonlit mountains. It is a city that cannot be tied down like trees by their roots. But (truth be told) it is an almost weightless city, with no roots, and it can be found in the lost tune of a rabab, or among the songs of a highwayman, or in a tale about the jinn. And if the Inner Monastery were the name of Qaddura's city, do I have a neighbourhood in this city? Or must I keep traveling in my 'innerhood' and 'outerhood' in search of the city of my name, and for my name as well, and then grant Qaddura himself a place in my city? The inhabitants of Rusaifa are originally Palestinian refugees from Haifa, Jaffa or Lydda, or . . . or . . . And if you were to ask any of them where he was from, he will say, 'I'm originally from Haifa, Jaffa or Lydda . . . or . . . or . .' In other words, he does not believe Rusaifa to be the city of his name, and indeed many of them have never known, and never seen, the city of their names or their origins, for it is a city that takes shape in the imagination, made up of the stories told by their mothers, fathers and grandfathers; or glimpsed in old photographs, old books, and so on . . . I never met anyone who considered Rusaifa to be the city of his name. This is the secret of Rusaifa itself: a vessel in which reside names that have lost their cities. They are names wandering around in the desert, like winds in the night-time, or in measureless time, and might pass by all the invisible cities in the world:

Every night I sing in a city
Then pick up my voice and start walking.

And you may some day reach the 'lost cities'. Who knows?

But Rusaifa, as I have already said, is a misunderstanding with God. It is a metropolis with no names that belong to it.

CHAPTER THREE

WHEN THE FOXES DO NOT ARRIVE

We built our dream, Áthar, Petra and I: a new house, small and white, in an olive orchard near the uncultivated summit of a mountain. This was the house of my name—'The House That Is the Last in Line.' I sit in the shadow of a moonlit olive tree on some bedding or on a straw stool, near 'the house that is near the sand' (as Áthar calls it), and gaze at the wadis. The obscure outline of trees that resemble primitive beings guards the line of the horizon separating the mountaintop from the sky. Every time I see this line, I think of Feiruz's song:

> The night and I were walking in silence
> When it said, I'll keep it dark for you
> Till you reach them, with no one seeing you.

When I lived in exile, I wrote a song about the line of the horizon that a highwayman sings to a she-lion whom God had forgotten in these wilds:

> Once the moon stood with me at the mountaintop
> My horse with me
> My thoroughbred, the shotgun and the aba
> the moustache curled

—Your uncle puts his heart in the moustache when he
    curls—
Standing alone like the trees, the dew freezing on my hair
Standing alone
The wind blowing from the north, thoughts from deep in
    the heart
Buried, that no one had seen
Seven (*sab 'a*) tears fell, and a tear
And tears are precious, O she-lion! (*sab 'a*). Listen
Your uncle's life is hard!
His horse is with him
His thoroughbred, the shotgun and the *aba*
He could never suffer loss of dignity in low-lying lands.

That was the line of the horizon in my imagination. Thirty
years of voluntary exile, and that was still the line of the horizon
in my imagination. And now, as I sit in the moonlit shadow of the
olive tree, I imagine the line of the horizon to be a ladder. The
ancient Pharaohs believed that the first sky was made of iron, and
whoever wanted to reach it had to do so from the mountaintops—
the ladders of the spirit. And now I am feeling a certain fear of
this line, and of the primitive and obscure shadows of the trees
on it. My mind is brimming with doubts. Who knows, for example, what dangerous powers are lurking in the invisible spot
between the ground and the moonlit shadows? A rogue viper, like
the one that bit Qaddura, may be turning over under my pillow.
Or pale scorpions that I cannot see could be breeding between
the moonlight and the ground. My mind sometimes overflows
with scorpions and vipers, and one is in need of strong willpower
to shout out:

I am not one of those who guard against
The bite of vipers, to sleep on top of scorpions.

Otherwise, the mind will sleep happily on its scorpions because it had saved itself from the vipers.

I have, and have not, returned to this Mountain. As if I had returned, but had not. There is no peace here, and I want to build a fence that will separate me from it. At the line of the horizon, the most domestic plants appear strange and primitive, without distinct features. And when the Mountain 'sings', what streams from it are the sounds of beasts I do not recognize, and others that I do, coming from the wadis and the line of the horizon: the barking of rabid dogs snapping at other animals; the knuckle bone from a pigeon's foot falling from a nest on the roof; foxes; the hissing of a weasel; the footsteps of wild cats; and the sound of a nay from the cave of memory. Above this strange, expressive music is a moon at the top of the Mountain, dark red and round, resembling the face of a goddess in quiet contemplation, her eyes closed as she listens to the buzzing of crickets that sounds like a soft background to this same strange, expressive music. Every note is whispering to me 'Don't sleep in the shadow of a moonlit olive tree in this spot of no-place. And don't hang around far from the house that is near the sand, because even the wild flowers are savage and will gash your feet, making them red like the redness of the moon.'

Because of the inflammation in my lungs and windpipe, when I breathe I produce sounds stranger than this 'singing of the Mountain'—a rattle that resembles a wounded mythical animal, and a clamour from the belly like the neighing of a horse, and so on. The sounds intermingle, as if there were a forest in my throat.

At first, I was able to distinguish the singing of the Mountain from the sounds I made, but recently I have experienced much confusion. The Mountain would be quiet, with the eyes of the red moon closed, and suddenly from the depths of the wadis strange sounds would erupt, belonging neither to the jinn nor to a human. I listen, and soon realize the sounds are coming from my own throat and chest. I can no longer make out the difference between the beasts of the Mountain and my vocal chords. Have I started to become wild, or to feel at home with wild animals? It seems as though the Mountain is in my belly, along with its misgivings. This calm moonlight may curdle into a scorpion, or, if I were to doze off and turn into a coloured viper that might break out of the trunk of the olive tree. Or, a hyena may come by and bite off what is left of me. And, who knows? Someone may assassinate me at this remote edge. I have returned; yet, I have not.

I stood at a dimly lit window in the house that is near the sand. By which window did I stand? At what period in time? And when was it that there was not? I do not know, except that I saw the olive tree from the perspective of that timeless time, and had the idea of this return to live in the countryside near Ramallah— a return with no coherent plot. Five foxes came by, some black and others close to red, and started to play under the same olive tree in the same spot where I had been. They played with the pillow for a while, dragging it here and there. Then they dragged the bed from under the tree to a spot in the middle of the emptiness. More accurately, they dragged the bedding to a spot in the no-place. I have returned, and have not, and the foxes realized that.

Every night was like that. A feeling would come over me of the disjointedness of the place, and my own disjointed perception of it. A weasel with the face of an owl came to rummage in a trash bag I had tossed away. Feral cats passed far from me, cautiously.

Once there came from the direction of the wadi a singing that sounded like a jinn wedding that then proceeded, with its nays and tambourines, or perhaps the screams of sea birds, up towards the line of the horizon.

This is not the 'mountain of memory' that I know but more like the 'mountain of gods'—a mountain that dreams jinn weddings, and dreams me. When the strange singing disappeared by the red face of the moon over the line of the horizon, a black fox appeared. It raised its ears, as if listening to the wind, and saw me under the olive tree. I was close to it, but it realized I was unable to attack, that I was from 'or there was not', so he passed me by as though I were less than a ghost. And in front of the house a weasel, standing on a stone in the mist of a pale yellow light, stretched its neck high in an attempt to see what was inside, then froze in place from its visions.

Disease, like time, shatters the sharp edges in all of us. I appeared to myself to be another red moonlit shadow standing on a rock at the line of the horizon that a gust of wind could blow away, or that a song could carry off.

The mountain may be all shadows to my mind and its anxieties, and I must learn the art of boxing with shadows, but in this desolate spot no one tests his sword against dust particles or chases moonbeams with a wooden spear. I sit and consider the power of the shadows that flow out of me and around me. It is not enough to build a new home. I must build a new spirit.

Thirty years in exile, and I am a fire worshipper from a tribe that roams the sea in ships. I am as I am, one of those who are as they are:

The course of rivers that seek no permanence
Roaming the world
Hoping the way may lead
To the path of deliverance from diaspora.

I returned to the house that is near the sand via 'the path of deliverance from diaspora'—a path that seemed to move in the direction of its outcome in a certain experience. Is this my ascent, I, the moonlit shadow near the line of the horizon, to the iron sky of the Pharaohs? Or is it my descent to the lowest point? Or did I return from an excess of energy—an energy bursting out of me— or from an excess of exhaustion?

I must return to the dormant child in me, so as to walk the earth as a child-prophet, if not in this life then in the next one. I glanced at Áthar, almost four years old now, as he played near me in the shadow of the moonlit olive tree. For some time I have been trying to learn from him how to return to the child-prophet dormant in us all. He saw the blinking red light of a plane, of the kind the Israelis are now using to liquidate the activists of the Intifada. It was passing near the moon, and blinking, like an electronic eye, like a houri. He asked, 'Hussein, this plane is from what?' 'From iron.' 'And is the moon afraid of iron?' 'Yes, yes. The moon is afraid of iron.'

Every child is a primitive magician, and has a staff like that of Moses, made of magical words. The first word Áthar spoke was *aeroplane*, followed by *moon*, followed by *crescent*. He used to say of the crescent that it 'drinks milk, and walks with me to his mother who is staying at the summit of the Mountain.' He constructed a fable with his words from the names of things as they appeared to his enchanted eyes. From *aeroplane*, *iron* and *fear* was born the fable of the 'moon that is afraid of iron'. An enchanting language for a more enchanting fable!

The child sees with enchanted eyes. An embryo soothsayer. Once when Áthar was young and could not speak yet, he was gazing at an obscure shadow between the chair and the wall in a room lit by candlelight. He tried to get away from me as though he had seen a miracle in the shadow. 'This is nothing but a shadow,' I teased him. 'There is nothing there.' He was too young to understand what I said. But a strange question occurred to me, 'What did I mean when I said this was nothing but a shadow, and there is nothing there?' It seemed to me I was blind, and that he could see whole worlds that I could not because I have become used to them. 'There is nothing there.' Who said that?

I have been observing his speech for some time. Once he heard me curse the power company because the lights had gone out. We were living in Birzeit then. There was heavy snow that brought down many of the pine and cypress trees in the woods. He looked through the window at the broken trees and cursed 'the snow company' and the 'cold company'. He saw a company in everything. The moon had a company, and the stars another.

He was asleep in my lap under the stars, moving his fingers and saying, 'I told you [feminine plural] don't play by yourselves in the street.' Then he said that his hand had left him and gone to the stars. Once I took him to the old city of Jerusalem, and he stood at the gateway of Khan al-Zeit street—a covered bazaar that looks like a labyrinth swarming with henna, gold, women tourists, Israeli soldiers, monks, and so on—and he started shaking with fear because he thought that the whole of Khan al-Zeit was an elevator reaching out horizontally, and he refused to enter.

From visions like these he builds his private fable. No one resembles anyone else in this world. Everything has its tale. And what is my tale of this place? I peer at the line of the horizon, my mind in flight. I ask myself, as though I were Áthar: 'Hussein, what's this?' And a voice from memory says, 'Line of the horizon, line of the horizon' And the child-prophet hidden within me asks. 'Fine. And what's this line of the horizon?'

I peer into the shadow of the moonlit olive tree and ask, 'Hussein, what's this?' And my memory answers, 'It's the moonlit shadow of an olive tree.' And the foxes of the Mountain answer,

'No. These are scorpions. A row of scorpions, but you insist it's the shadow of moonlit olive tree. There's no intelligence in your heart.'

Bring us back, O ancient sea, to 'the green mantle of the mermaids in the ashes and the visions of our poets!' Forget, O Hussein, those loved ones who died in travel by sea and became coral trees in the depths, and go back to your beginnings.

Áthar's sign is Pisces. A watery sign, changeable and artistic by nature.

Some time ago he accompanied me to Paris. There, at the house of the filmmaker Francois Abu Salem, I heard recordings of the songs of blue whales.

The blue whale is amazing. The tongue of a young blue whale is heavier than an elephant. They have follicles on top of their head that they use as antennas to detect the magnetic waves of the earth's gravity. Their sensitivity to gravity is 25 million times greater than that of human beings. These mammals sing in the depths of the ocean, passing sailors who have drowned and become trees of coral. With more than 400 variations, the singing sounds as though it were emerging from the bottom of the universe, and from an anxiety that even magicians cannot dream of. All this awakened in me a feeling I had never felt before from the Canaanite days of the *Enuma Elish*, when there were no names yet for the sky and the earth, and the universe was mere chaos.

The sign of the blue whale, to me, is a water sign. In it are four kinds of inspiration. Lorca distinguished four types of artistic inspiration.

In Arab culture, when God inspires a singer, the audience exclaims, 'Allah! Allah! What mastery!' The Arabs of old called this state of musical ecstasy ṭarab. There used to be in Petra a temple that was like the Temple of Dionysus—god of wine, intoxication, dancing, music and rapture, who made the vine sprout from the wood of a ship. The Arabs used the word baṭara [he became ecstatic] for someone touched by the madness of Dionysus, in reference to Petra, which they pronounced as baṭra', and which eventually became ṭarab.

But in Italy inspiration is angelic, and angels are innocent to the point of dullness, a blank state that does not yet know good or evil, resembling 'soft rain in a distant autumn'. For the Greeks, inspiration comes from the moon. The nine Muses are the sources of inspiration for the singer, blowing their breaths into his mouth. Thus Homer, for example, begins the *Odyssey* by asking the Muses to inspire him, or even to sing in his place. Yet their breath is cold, and they grant Lorca only 'half a heart of marble'! Marble does not dance, and should not. Maybe it has a rational quality—rigid, straight lines, angles and geometries. A cold inspiration!

As for inspiration in Spain, its name is Duende, and it is demonic, like pulverized glass in the blood, because the dead in Spain are more dead than any other dead in the world and there is no place in the world where death is a public spectacle as it is in the Spanish bullfight. Death and love overwhelm the spirit there, as Lorca said in 'Poem of the Deep Song':

> The dagger
> enters the heart
> the way plowshares turn over
> the wasteland
> *No.*
> *Do not cut into me.*
> *No.*

Like a ray of sun,
the dagger
ignites terrible
hollows.
No.
Do not cut into me.
No.

The sign of the blue whale (Pisces), as I said, is watery. In it is
a breath of all these kinds of inspiration, even the daemonic
Duende. Pisces feels with all his being, as though his brain were
in the inner parts of his heart; and if he were to write, he would
write with blood. And that, as Nietzsche says, is the best writing:
'Write with blood, and you will experience that blood is spirit.'
This inspiration takes from the Muses the sensitivity to propor-
tion, limits and order—of the kind that made Leonardo da Vinci
(I think), after having carved a statue that captivated people with
the beauty of its nose, break the nose with a hammer because he
wanted to carve a beautiful statue and not only a beautiful nose.
Pisces longs to overflow the scope of any limit, scale or order.
There is in it also a supernatural sensitivity, a possession by freedom. We find this sensitivity, for example, in the music of Ziad
al-Rahbani. There is in it that which makes Arab people cry out,
'Allah! Allah! What mastery!' In it also is the whiteness of snow
and the purity of angels.

You will always find it playing at the transparent edge between the
nameable and the un-nameable, going back in time to Canaanite
days when earth and sky did not yet have names, and the universe
was still in chaos. It is the zodiac sign of the child-prophet.

The child-prophet is not a child but a blue whale swimming
in the depths among seamen who have turned into coral. Complex

labyrinths taught him dancing; that is, he matured, then turned into a child again. Among his names are 'the Genius' in Baudelaire and the Soothsayer in Rimbaud.

He loves life more than it is possible for anyone to imagine. He resembles the last shot of the film *Blade Runner*—in which the human being/machine is on the roof of a skyscraper in a downpour, with only a few seconds left to live. His worst enemy—who may be human—is gripping his hand. And he says to that enemy: 'I will not kill you, because I love life more than you could possibly imagine.' Then he opens his hand to the raining sky, and out fly flocks of doves that are white, white, white. Lord, how white were those doves! His astrological sign, to me, is 'the blue Pisces'.

* * *

Once Francois visited us in the house near the sand. He found a shrivelled ear of wheat on the Mountain and gave it to Áthar, asking, 'What's this?' Áthar thought for a moment as he turned it over, and said, 'This? This is for ringing the bell.' 'Which bell?' 'The bell of the world.' 'And what does the bell of the world sound like?' Áthar laughed, and made the sound of an ambulance siren he had heard when he came to visit me at the Ramallah hospital.

The child, according to his first and primitive nature, sees the world in a gyre. This is art. Lorca says that art is swerving, as in the bullfight; for, what idiot would throw himself at the bull's horns? Rather, art is the matador throwing himself at the bull's horns, then swerving at the last moment. This Mountain is a bull's horn, and I must swerve from it at the last moment. I must see it in a gyre, like a child.

Like Áthar, I have started to imagine the Mountain as a bell made of red brass and turned upside down, with all its plants and rocks cast in bronze and shining under a red moon that is like the

face of a goddess who rings the bell with closed eyes. And I imagined that it would ring if Áthar and I were to walk on it near the
line of the horizon, as though we were ears of wheat ringing the
bell of the world. The Mountain would then be free of its weight,
and would ring and ring, as if our steps were a bronze clapper in
the hands of one of the great musicians of the jinn. Enchanted by
its ringing, the ghreriyas would flock to it, as would foxes, vipers,
people and all the beings that live on it, and listen to the new
music of a memory that goes back to their beginnings. And the
Mountain would reach within them like the sounds of the wild
animals reaching into my larynx.

Yes, yes, yes. As long as I cannot distinguish among the
sounds that rise from my larynx and chest, and the sounds of the
wild animals here, I mean, as long as the voice of the Mountain
reaches into my chest like the reach of the olive into the oil, then
I am the Mountain, and the Mountain is me, and together we are
the bell of the world, 'the telegram of wheat in the meadow of lead'.

And because I am partial to wheat, I took Áthar by the hand
and we walked towards the line of the horizon, wanting to go deep
into that which brings us fear, into the 'iron' of which the moon
is afraid, that we may forge from it our return to Qaddura's nay,
or his rabab, with daring.

Suddenly, he heard the strange sound of a wild animal. 'Hussein, what's this?' 'I don't know.' Afraid, he took my hand. 'Go
back, go back!' So we went back. My return has failed! On that
same night that I am talking about, the foxes dragged my bedding
to the very spot at which he said, 'Go back! Go back!'

I turned on the radio to listen to the news. The settlers were
burning a mountain of olive trees in a village in the north. I imagined the scene: smoke and fire, the wind scattering them in the
horizon and the glow lighting up the wadis, in another version—

and of a different sort—of the film *Red Desert*. Áthar said, 'Don't let the radio talk loud.' 'Why?' 'A snake will come out of it!' OK. OK. I put on a cassette. 'Hussein, there's a cricket in this music.' O God, save us from the house that is near the sand! I have returned; yet, I have not.

* * *

No one returns to his beginnings, even occasionally, unless he goes to his history, to himself in his history. I mean to say, I was searching for a city for my name. And only in history is it possible for any name to have its city: In Petra, for example, this city that ancient Arab carvers of time have carved in rose-coloured rocks.

There, while sitting with Petra and Áthar in front of the columns of the Treasury, looking at a huge guard dog and a tourist who likes to take pictures mounted on a camel covered with a Bedouin rug embroidered with geometrical shapes, I felt I was the son of this heritage, and my spirit fluctuated in facing it between rocks and ashes, between the Pyramids and the songs that pass. From this place came the Nabatean alphabet, from which descended the Arabic alphabet that I am now using to write. They carved a city in rock, and another in the alphabet. And I? I am one of those born 'outside time'. All that has remained for me is a camel and a tourist riding it with a camera around his neck.

'What a loss,' I thought, 'that you should pass over the surface of the earth and not change anything, or leave any trace. What a loss, O son of this great heritage! What a loss that you should be born in a time of defeat, with the awareness of defeat and fear! Even the name of your son Áthar was thought to be Arthur, a foreign name, a name coming from those who colonized you. No one even considered that it comes from the Arabic language. What a loss that you should lose your identity to such an extent!'

Is this a forced flight away from history, or into it—that was what made me search for the city of my name without finding it. Was that the secret of the vagrancy of my name itself?

At the entrance to Petra I paid a very high admission fee that is usually paid only by foreign tourists. In vain did I try to convince the employee selling tickets that I was not a 'foreigner' to my heritage or to his. When someone loses his past, you can shape his future any way you want because he has lost the shadow that reaches back in history. This colourful rock in Petra is my shadow—I, whose fate is only to observe, to look and pass, and not interfere or carve or even protest—someone who suffers from an inflamed swelling, a flood of red cells in the left lobe of his lung.

From this heritage only my body is left; rather, the remains of a body. Remains that resemble Feiruz's song:

O tree of time, the wind has changed us!
It tore up our leaves and left us naked
O tree, waiting alone where the wind blows
Like you, I'm a tree at a crossroads.

This is the song of someone who has stripped himself of his history, or who has had it stripped from him, one who feels under this moonlit olive tree that he is 'outside time', alone, without a dream, only the reflection of a dream. The difference here is the letter 'r' by which Áthar becomes Arthur. As long as the present is the horn of the bull, I have to swerve in order to see straight.

For some time now I have been flying like a bird, blown at an angle by the wind and having to swerve in order to see. Before I was introduced to my wife Petra, for example, in the studio where I was living in Ramallah, I used to watch my shadow on the wall at night by the light of a candle. I would feel that I was the shadow, and that the shadow was me. Or maybe it was the shadow that did the watching, and I was one-dimensional, flat, like the pre-Islamic soothsayer, Satih who used to fold his body like a robe that could be placed inside a wardrobe.

When the power was off, darkness covered everything. It covered all my shadows, and only a body remained: a mute shadowless mass. I would run my hands over it as though it were a wall of coarse cement. Even my hair felt as though it grew out of my skin like chrysanthemums and ears of wheat, as if I were a field or an archaeological mound. Is this not, then, a nostalgia for history?

One night, I stood in front of the mirror in the bathroom in my studio under a faint yellow electric light and gazed at my face as though I were another person.

My hair was blond, very long, and frizzy, the braids running down to my shoulders. It was wet and the water was dripping from it onto my eyes and eyebrows and lips. Suddenly I saw myself as a very old man, the thick eyebrows and bones turned fragile from age; a head lit up with grey hair; and thick, very red, lips and strange eyes peering into the invisible but not seeing what was in front of them. I felt I was Tiresias, the oracle of Delphi in the Fourth Century BCE. I was not of this age, and I began to recite lines from T. S. Eliot's *The Wasteland*: 'I, Tiresias, saw all of this.'

I came out of the bathroom into a courtyard planted with almonds, lemons and the stars around the studio, repeating, 'I, Tiresias, saw all of this.' And I saw Ramallah, daughter of this deranged history, and said: 'I am the only witness, God be my witness!'

Petra came into the courtyard, and we met each other among the almond trees. We married, and I was diagnosed with cancer. My hair began to fall from the chemotherapy. I stood in front of another mirror in another house, on another night, and under another light in Birzeit and touched my hair. It was dry, like fine metal strings, yet I could not feel it. Every time my hand touched one of my braids, some of the hair came out between my fingers or fell into the sink. 'And, I, Tiresias, saw all of this.' I thought, Go back to your history. 'Alone,' Shakespeare said. 'You are nothing.' Even Tiresias was the official spokesman of the gods. He was not alone.

I shaved my head, and a baldness broke forth that shone in the yellow light like a new identity anointed with olive oil. I was a more mature Tiresias. I did not know what was my name now, nor the city of my name. I chuckled at my shape, my being I, my being here and what I must become.

In the eyes of others, I may have been seen as the one with the long, blond hair, a mere rebel whose revolt did not go beyond the length of his hair. And now a bald man has emerged, a man who has lost his distinguishing mark. My identity comes from my history and my spirit, and not from my hair or my baldness. But they have deprived me of my history, and I remain nothing more than a tree at a crossroads. And now cancer is trying to undress me even of my skin?

I thought as I stared into the mirror that all I needed was a long yellow robe, fit for a soothsayer or a child-prophet, an ancient sandal made of leather and immense toenails suitable even for tramping in swamps. I needed to depart in search of a name for myself, and a city for my name within the history of this spot in history. I would visit the Egyptian Thebes, Babylon, Palmyra, Petra and Andalusia, even if my sandals were nothing more than a white lily in a footprint of ruin.

For a time, and only to myself, I called myself Tiresias. I changed my name and city of residence according to the occasion. At one time I was Marduk, the most powerful Babylonian god; at other times I was the poet Imru' al-Qays, or a youth reciting poetry in the taverns of Aleppo during the time of the Abbasids; or a black slave, taking part in the Zanj Rebellion in the Middle Ages, who was bought by a beautiful woman from Isfahan. Another time I visited Siduri, the tavern keeper in the epic of *Gilgamesh*, and I was also a vagrant with the poet Ta'abbata Sharran, who:

> Deemed solitude fellowship itself, and found his path
> As the mother of the intertwining stars finds hers.

Some other time I was standing with two Roman servants in front of a palace in Egypt when Cleopatra lost the Battle of Actium. A procession passed, singing about an imaginary victory:

> Our victory at Actium
> Is famous all around
> Ask the Roman fleet
> If we had not given it a taste of destruction

I heard one of the servants commenting on the song to his friend in Ahmad Shawqi's play, *The Death of Cleopatra*:

> Listen to the crowd, Dion
> How they do incite it!
> O what parrots the people are
> With their brains in their ears!

Lord, how alone I felt at times, as though I were the poet who roamed desolate regions with no trace of living beings. And suddenly:

> The wolf howled, and I was at ease with the wolf as it
>   howled
> [But when] a human being made a sound I almost flew
>   away.

And so on, and so forth. Then in my travels I realized I was not my hair, even if it were to drop off one braid after the other;

and not my body, even if they were to burn it in a Buddhist fire or place it in a zinc urn and say, 'These are your ashes, cry for them.' There must be love, and there must be beauty. 'Beauty will not save the world, but beauty must be saved in this world,' a certain writer said.

After thirty years of voluntary exile from the Mountain, I returned to it, to a beauty that I had forgotten or had even betrayed. Who among the people of this countryside knows that I have been in the Egyptian Thebes and consorted with the priests of the temple at Karnak; that I have witnessed a wild pig killing the god Adonis in the shade of the pines in the woods of Lebanon and seen his blood turning into red anemone flowers; that I have slept in Mesopotamia with a holy prostitute at the cold spring near the city of Uruk, then drunk wine and eaten the bread of Uruk because that was how things were done there? Who knows where I have been? No one. And no one will know where I will go!

Finally, I find myself in the house that is near the sand. Every night the foxes drag my bedding from under the moonlit olive tree into the middle of the emptiness. For some nights now, I have not thrown any food in their direction nor put out the garbage in a plastic bag. So for some nights the foxes have not been coming. I felt isolated. Strange how isolated I feel. We could have become friends, the foxes and the weasel peering every night and the feral cats and the vipers and the scorpions and I, and we could have walked together to the line of the horizon. We could have done that, except that the foxes have not come for some nights. I feel sad, and wait for them to return.

* * *

I remained seated in a straw chair in moonlit shadow—a shadow from the time of the Byzantines (the olive trees are from those times)—listening to an obscure performance on the nay until morning broke. A very white mist appeared as if it had congealed at the bottom of the wadis. My skin was bathing in a refreshing bite of cold. The sun was beginning to rise, the birds began to sing in the orchards, the ants were on the wing and life was waking.

Near the house that is near the sand, a path in the fig orchards paved with white pebbles appeared to be lit by the moon, perhaps from the redness of the soil around them. Suddenly I became aware of something brown that appeared and then disappeared on the path. I gazed deeply into the dark light and saw a strange animal that I had never seen before—a stranger to the Mountain. Like me, its colour was dark red, closer to brown, the hair on its back like a comb with bristles, and high front legs. A hyena, O God! Sooner or later, it will snatch Áthar away and devour him. But a doubt about what I was seeing gripped me. Hyenas are the Mountain's legends. And this creature is a stranger to the Mountain. It was not a hyena. I peered more closely.

Behind it was a smaller animal, its offspring perhaps. Dark red, closer to brown, its face submerged in the dew on the path— it was sniffing around. It then occurred to me that I had seen a creature like this in the book *Hunting in Art*. This was a wild boar! But what if it were a hyena?

I was exhausted from the swelling in the left lobe of my lung, which had increased to 37 square centimetres. Merely walking ten steps exhausted me. I would not have been able to defend myself, or Áthar. I walked towards this creature, free of any aggressive intent. I wanted to see its face, whether it was a hyena or a boar, completely forgetting that I was myself an easy prey in either case.

It seemed the love of discovery for its own sake had taken over and was driving me relentlessly to my death. I walked towards the animal with an innocence that approached foolishness. As I drew closer, it became aware of me. It raised its head high and peered at me from the middle of the fig trees, but I did not see its face clearly. I tried to see; only see. And suddenly, it lunged, clawing and scattering the red soil with its hooves, head down. With one butt of that head it could crack open a tree trunk.

I stayed put. Its movements seemed comical, disjointed, as though it were a calf and not a wild animal. I laughed at the way it moved. It lunged with all its body but was only ten steps from me it came to a stop. I was still trying to make out its face. It raised its head and ears higher, and we gazed at each other. It seemed as if it had smelt my intentions. Intentions have a smell, like fear and perspiration, and it could not tell what I wanted. I too could not tell what it wanted from me. I focused on its face with absolute innocence. It grew more bewildered. I looked at its young, a tiny reddish animal walking peacefully on the white path behind it, still sniffing the dirt. And I understood: it too was defending its young, wanting to be reassured about the safety of the one who may have a 'house that is near the figs'.

We stood for a while among the fig trees and gazed at each other and then I remembered Áthar again. I turned around and returned from where I had come. And when I looked back, I noticed it too had turned and gone away. I looked through the window at Áthar and his mother. They were sleeping peacefully. I wanted to wake them up so they could see our new friends. I looked at the brown boar again; it was walking with its young one, completely forgotten that we had met. Yet it was possible that we could have become friends.

* * *

I then turned to my own special world. I was trying to imagine Qaddura, my mother's uncle, as he played his rabab on the roof of the Inner Monastery, looking over deep moonlit wadis, and the ploughed and planted orchards. I was trying to imagine him as he lit the fire at night and smoked his narghile, my mother having brought him the embers in a pair of tongs.

I had asked her, under the moonlit olive tree: 'Did anyone ever come to visit him?'

'Yes. Yes. People used to trust each other more than they do today. They expected more from each other. We used to leave the key on the lintel above the door, and a big clay jar full of water outside for whoever may come by in case they needed a drink.'

'And who used to visit him?'

'The gypsies.'

'Gypsies?'

'Yes.'

'And did they sing and dance on the Mountain around a fire, with their horses nearby, eating their fodder?'

'No. No. I heard from the elders of our tribe that a gypsy woman used to come and do some rope walking, and sing. Also a man with a monkey that danced in a comical manner. And someone with a magic box he used to accompany his recitation of the Beni Hilal epic. And fortune-tellers. I was young then, and remember that the gypsies of the Inner Monastery were gazelle hunters. They set their traps and sat up with Qaddura on the roof of the monastery.'

'And what did he do when he sat up with them?'

'He played his rabab and sang from the epic of *Al-Zīr Sālim.*'

* * *

The gypsies of Palestine say they are ancient Arabs from the Jassas Quarter, and that Al-Zīr Salem drove them out of the Naqab desert. They called them nawar in relation to al-nūr [light], or perhaps al-nār [fire]. What did they see at night at the Inner Monastery when they gazed into the fire and listened to the epic tale of *Al-Zīr Sālim*? The city of their names? And did Qaddura's rabab take them back on its one string to their origins?

When I was a child, a gypsy fortune-teller used to come to our house. She wore colourful clothes and had a green tattoo on her chin. She had conches and white seashells that she threw on the floor to read fortunes. I was fascinated by the strangeness of her world. Decades later, when I lived in Hungary, I visited gypsy taverns and listened to their songs. I loved the poetry of Károly Bari:

O my seven brothers
Whom the winds have scattered at night over seven rocks
Over you I lay my only shirt

The soothsayer is still sitting at the time of my beginnings, scattering shells on the floor and reading the shapes they form:

Where are you from?
I'm from the country of tales

That the gypsy fantasy may continue, my father called me 'the gypsy', and my mother said one day that the gypsies had brought me with them as a baby. And just as they gazed into the fire at the Inner Monastery, its glow shining on their wrinkled faces, remembering the origin of their names and their stories in the tales of *Al-Zir Salem*, I too gaze into the memories of my mother about them, and about Qaddura's rabab. I stumble upon them in my memory before I was born. I mean, my beginnings do no start from a point but from a shining star!

Decades later I would write 'Gypsy Song': 'My origin's a gypsy / and that's my fate' and 'I live on old things, selling horses, antique coins, silver anklets, and tales.' I also participated in a documentary film about these 'strangers'. It opens with a shot of a gypsy woman much like the old soothsayer, with a tattoo on her chin and lips, smoking in front of an obscure fire, and in a deep and gravelly voice foretelling the difficult times to come—a prophecy from the epic of *Al-Zir Salem*. Yet the encounters between Arab and gypsy cultures are older than this. It is said that the gypsies reached Spain in 1477 CE at a time when the Arabs ruled Andalusia. And from Andalusian folk songs, Byzantine Christian canticles, the songs of the Sefardim and Muslim Arabs, and the songs of the mysterious gypsies, a writhing kind of song developed, with a deep spiritual colouring. It was called 'the deep song' [*cante jondo*], and from there came flamenco music.

Lorca wrote *Poem of the Deep Song* drawing inspiration from these depths—which belong to us Arabs and the gypsies—about two rivers in Granada: The first one weeps and the second is running with blood; also a river with a beard made of garnets. And about an

Ancient
land of oil lamps
and grief.
Land of deep cisterns.
Land of death without eyes
and arrows

And also about blind women staring at the moon, and so on.

I love the poetry of Lorca. Before Áthar was born at the Red Crescent hospital in Ramallah, I thought of calling him Lorca so that he could travel to the city of his name and reach Andalusia. His name will then be like the red moon that resembles a goddess contemplating the Mountain with her eyes closed, and will hover over his dreams. A gypsy soothsayer will arrive and with a voice like that of the houris sing to him these lines from Mahmoud Darwish:

I'll come to you as I do every night
Open the window in a dream, and throw you a carnation.

She will then give him 'a white shell that resembles this pale moon appearing to be a shell washed by the waters of time when it rises and falls among the stars and then breaks into minutes and years.' That shell will smell like a woman and sea salt, and of something else that, were he to smell it, will take his spirit to the Alhambra palace in Andalusia, and to a river with a garnet beard. And it will spread from Alhambra to Petra, and from Babylon to the Temple at Karnak, and from the gypsies to Al-Zir Salem.

'And where are you from
I'm from the country of windows'

My beginnings are not from a point but from a star that shines. And among its rays are the gypsies who knew my mother, Qaddura, his narghile, his rabab and the Inner Monastery, and their origins in his stories about al-Zir Salem. And all these belong to the history of which I have been stripped, or which they have denuded me of. What a loss, O son of this great heritage!

Who knows where I have come from? No one. And no one will know where I will go. I passed by the Deep Song as a soothsayer wearing a yellow robe in which all the rivers meet so that Áthar will be a fairy tale.

Once, in the nineteenth century, I sat with the American poet Edgar Allan Poe as he was writing a poem with the Arabic title, 'Al Aar[r]af' ['the soothsayer']: 'All Nature speaks, and ev'n ideal things / Flap shadowy sounds from visionary wings.' And I dreamt of the Siwa Oasis in the Libyan Desert, the location of the Temple of Ammon Ra, where it is said that Alexander the Great was buried. It has also been said that Alexander was himself of Egyptian origins. I have roots in Egypt, and in the Two-Horned Alexander.

It is also said that Nectanebus was a magician who ruled Egypt around 358 BCE. He was a soothsayer and astrologer with the ability to make people dream. When, for example, enemies attacked Egypt by sea, his custom was to enter a special chamber in his palace, set aside for magical practices, and make small waxen statues of his friends and enemies and put them in a vessel full of water. He would then put on the robe of an Egyptian prophet, hold an ebony rod in his hand, and call upon the gods of Egypt, among whom are 'Amon', or 'Amen', to drown with the power of magic words his enemies in the sea or in the vessel—no difference. One day, not one single statue drowned, because the Egyptian gods fought on the side of his enemies, and he realized that his kingdom was about to fall. He disguised himself as an ordinary human being and escaped in a ship to Macedonia and there lived as an Egyptian priest and soothsayer.

In Macedonia, he sent a dream to the mother of Alexander the Macedonian, Olympia, revealing to her that the Egyptian god Amon will come to her in a dream and have intercourse with her, whereupon she will become pregnant with a male human and retain the memory that he is the son of Amon. Olympia became pregnant, and when she was in labour, 'Nectanebus stood by her making observations of the heavenly bodies, and from time to time he besought her to restrain herself until the auspicious hour had arrived. And it was not until he saw a certain splendour in the sky and he knew that all the heavenly bodies were in a favourable position that he allowed her to bring forth her child.

And when he said, "Now, now, O queen, now thou wilt give birth to the governor of the world," the child fell upon the ground . . .'

In those days, an occult unity had formed between two Pharaonic deities: 'Ra' (Sun-God), and 'Amon'. One of the symbols of Amon-Ra is the golden eagle. It is said that Nectanebus sent an 'eagle' to the dream world of Philip, husband of Olympia, informing him that Alexander was not his son but the son of Amon.

Alexander the Macedonian conquered the ancient world, and built Alexandria. Then he melted, like others, into the folklore of this part of the world, including the heritage of Palestine. Alexander remained anxious about his identity. Who was he exactly? So he went to a soothsayer at the Siwa Oasis in the Libyan Desert to uncover the truth about his origin, and the soothsayer said he was the son of the god Amon, and not the son of Philip. And because the roots of the cult of Amon are in moon worship, Alexander believed he was a lunar god. The currency he issued showed his image with horns (like the moon). He started to ask his followers to prostrate themselves to him in worship. He died in Egypt, and it is said that his corpse was moved to the Siwa Oasis, where the Temple of Amon-Ra is to be found.

A while ago I saw a television report about an archaeologist who was digging in the oasis in search of his place of burial, but as a French artist whom I met in Le Dive told me, they stopped her dig and put a fence around the whole area.

I mean it is banal to consider a person as the son of his father and mother, Nietzsche says. I can be the son of Alexander the Great, as Alexander himself was the son of Amon and not of Philip. And I can also be the son of Ptolemy or Al-Mutanabbi, or Jalaluddin Rumi, or the Deep Song, or the string of a rabab. To swerve away from the bull's horns, I say it is banal that a person should be the son of their mother and father.

Then I met those who have returned and did not return to the Mountain, and 'they are as they are, the course of rivers that seek no permanence'. And here I am, after all this journeying, in a small house, painted white, with my son and my wife. And I am he, this person sitting in the shadow of a moonlit olive tree, the one whose bedding the foxes dragged to a spot in the emptiness. I am he, he himself. And this house that is 'near the sand', is the house of this person; he himself. An olive tree protects him—the one whose mother gave birth to in 'the warm orchard guarded by a green stone'. This is he, himself; not a legend or pure imagination, but a folktale from the tales of this Mountain and the Inner Monastery, and

I see . . .

I see what I want of the ladder.

And this seventy-year-old woman is my mother, absorbed in planting garlic, tomatoes and native onions in primitive planters made of stone around the house that is near the sand—the very same kinds of crops she used to plant at the Inner Monastery before she was married, and before my father planted the orchards for her around our house with almond trees. She is reverting to her memories, brimming with life, and I have been cured of cancer. She is planting for me and Áthar and Petra all the ingredients of the salad that will be a celebration of life. And in spring, among the bees, the almond blossoms, the line of ants, the sun and the birds, I will learn how to play the rabab. I will sit on the roof of our house and play, exactly like Qaddura, and look over deep moonlit valleys and planted and ploughed orchards, and with all of this I will have completed another cycle in the eternal cycle of reincarnation and another fairy tale of the mountain. Another cycle, and another fairy tale! My beginnings go back to a shining star, and my endings also.

And one day the Mountain will realize that it had chosen permanence, like the city of Petra, while I have opted for motion, like fire and air and songs and folktales and tales of the jinn, and we are bound to meet again, even if only in a rabab's tune.

The Mountain is my first beginning, and I pushed it to its utmost limits: I made it reach Alexander the Macedonian, and Al-Mutanabbi and Amon and Ra and the Cape of Good Hope and Lao Tzu and Buddha and Rumi and Baudelaire and Marquez and Mishima, and many such others—many, many others. And in me it has reached as far as it could reach, and it, it became itself. I am more conscious of my beginning. Will this Mountain itself, then, recognize in the features of my face that are starting to turn into a strange myth indeed—one of its furthest reaches and one of its endings? I am one of its ghreriyas, and the time has arrived for it now to see me in the guise of a badger going up, walking up towards the red moon that resembles a goddess contemplating the line of the horizon with her eyes closed, saying to me, 'Over there, over there, do you not see? Over there—the ladders of the spirit ascending to the iron sky of the Pharaohs! Go up!'

May God be my witness! May God be my witness! And may the Mountain sing!

TRANSLATOR'S NOTES

The Arabic title of this memoir is *Sa'akūnu bayn al-Lawz* (literally, *I'll Be Among the Almond Trees*).

I have used the Arabic original for words that now need no definition in English, like keffiyeh and aba (men's garment in Palestine, though used with reference to women's outer cloak in other Arab countries), without diacritical marks. In these notes, on the other hand, I render all Arabic words in Modern Standard Arabic; hence the difference between deir, which is how the word is pronounced in the spoken Arabic of Palestine, and the MSA equivalent—al-Dayr. All Arabic words are transliterated according to the system recommended by the Library of Congress.

Concerning text in quotation marks, I have supplied the sources when I could find them.

CHAPTER ONE: THE 'INNER MONASTERY'

Page 35 | 'The "Inner Monastery"'—Later in the memoir, Barghouthi provides an impressionistic explanation for the use of the word 'inner' (juwwānī) for the monastery. The Arabic word deir can refer to a number of religious institutions, most commonly to a parish (church, priest, and parish house). It can also refer to a monastery, an abbey, a convent or priory. I have opted for 'monastery' because, in imagining monks walking contemplatively in the courtyard, the author obviously thinks of it as such. Additionally, all such ruins in Palestine are understood by archaeologists to have been Byzantine monasteries. An indication of the prevalence of these monasteries (or parishes) that once existed in the country is the large number of towns and villages, before 1948 and after, that have a name beginning with Deir, including the village of Deir Ghassaneh (the ancestral home of the Barghouthis). The actual deir referred to sits on top of a mountain far from the village of Kobar, where the action takes place. As we shall see further on, this mountain is one of the heroes of this narrative.

'my last Wailing Wall'—Reference here is to the Second (or al-Aqsa) Intifada (2000–2005). Most of the websites dedicated to this subject ignore the overwhelming fact of Palestinian life under occupation that led to the first and second intifadas—the Israeli occupation that began in 1967. The occupation hangs over this narrative in the form of settlements and helicopters and the resistance to it in the First and Second Intifadas. The most accurate description of the Second Intifada is to be found at www.just-vision.org/glossary/second-intifada.

Page 37 | 'a "rogue" snake struck Qaddura's right foot'—The Palestine Viper (*Daboia palaestinae*), a colourful and very poisonous snake.

Page 39 | 'the last ghreriya in the mountains'—Ghrerīya (colloquial Palestinian). In his Introduction to the Arabic edition, the Palestinian poet Ahmad Dahbour notes that Barghouthi's naming is unusual because he knows this animal as the ghurayrī (that is, belonging to the species, ghurayr—the badger), which is not extinct in Palestine. I have kept the author's version of the name because he evinces a strong enough identification with this animal to suggest that his soul will transmigrate into one after his death. He is also fascinated by the sound of its name, and will later engage in word play based on it.

Page 40 | 'highwayman playing the nay'—The spike-fiddle rabab (rabāba), is a folk instrument that usually has one string. The nay is an open-ended reed flute. The author, further on, uses quotation marks around the word *females* to draw attention to the fact that the rabab is a 'female' only to the extent that the grammatical gender of the word in Arabic (a gendered language) is feminine. The yoking of a female human with the feminine gender of the rabab is a way of injecting language into the fabric of reality.

Page 45 | 'They bring me the arak . . . they say'—Arak is usually drunk with water, which turns it cloudy white; hence the apt comparison of the grey hair and the white arak. Unfortunately, the rhyme that links the two parts of this (most likely) improvised line of folk song (*fi-l-kāsī*: 'in the glass', *rāsī*: 'my head') was lost in translation.

Page 46 | 'Live for your body . . . not your dream!'—Barghouthi here abridges several lines from Darwish's poem 'Mural', about his near-death experience: 'All is vanity. Take hold / of your life as it is, a moment pregnant with its fluid, / the distilled blood of the grass. / Live for the day! Not / for your dream. Everything passes. Be careful tomorrow, but today / Live inside a woman / who loves you. Live for your body, not your illusions.'—*Mural* (Beirut: Riad El-Rayyes Books, 2000), p. 84.

Page 47 | 'the ghūla's lantern'—The Arabic word ghūl (fem. ghūla) does not refer to the same imaginary being denoted by the English word *ghoul*, who is understood to be a 'legendary evil being that robs graves and feeds on corpses'. Ghūls are characters in Arabic folktales that often serve as helper figures. Though they are thought of as monsters, they share many qualities with human beings. Ghūls are not very intelligent, and can be easily hoodwinked by a clever hero (or heroine). In fact the ability to outwit a ghūl is part of the test of heroism. Ghūls are selfish and greedy while ghūlas have strong motherly instincts and can be pacified by suckling at the breasts that are so huge they can be flung over their shoulders. If it is necessary for a hero or heroine to kill a ghūla, it must be done with only one strike of the sword. To deceive the hero into thinking that another blow will be the end of her, the ghūla asks to be struck a second time. At that point, the correct response to that request is: 'My mother didn't teach me how', for a second blow would revive her. (For further examples of ghūl behaviour, see Muhawi and Kanaana, Tales 16, 18, 19, 20, 22, among others.) Barghouthi seems fascinated with these supernatural (or sub-natural) creatures, and I think they form part of the intermingling of the familiar and the wild that animates this work, including the cancer in his body which is an internal ghūl with its own uncontrollable growth and which he tries to pacify by means of the various treatments to which he is subjected.

'The Goulah's Lantern' (*Sirāj al-Ghūlah*) is the folk name for a lilac-coloured flower with six petals that appears for only a few days after the first rains in October. It is not the firefly described by the author, which is called *sirāj al-layl* ('the lantern of the night'). The scientific name for *sirāj al-ghūlah* is *Colchicum stevenii*, or 'Steven's meadow saffron'. English: en.wikipedia.org/wiki/Colchicum

Page 48 | 'Lord Khader the Green and Lord Jesus'—In Palestinian and general Arabic folklore, al-Khader (Christian: St George) is the Islamic version of what in Europe is known as 'the Green Man'. In folklore, he is presented as an immortal avatar, a figure that helps people in need, as he does in the legend narrated by the author's mother. As we can see from the story in which he is described as travelling with Jesus rather than Moses, as in the Qur'an, his legends are still current in Palestine. The stories of al-Khader are told in the surah of the Cave (*Al-Kahf*), verses 64–82, where he accompanies the Prophet Moses on a journey, acting as his guide. For folk stories about al-Khader in Palestine, see Hanauer, Chapter 9.

Page 49 | 'lead the herd to the Qteiliya'—In the Palestinian dialect, Qteilīya is the diminutive form of al-Qatīla—the woman who was killed.

Page 53 | 'The mountain! O Sariya, the mountain!'—A reference to an Islamic legend, which some authorities say was an actual event that took place in 645 CE. The story concerns the Caliph Umar Ibn al-Khattab, who, during the course of a sermon from the pulpit of the Prophet, exclaimed, 'The mountain, O Sariya, the mountain! He who makes of the wolf a shepherd is an oppressor.' Asked about the meaning of his exclamation, Umar said he did not know how he came to utter it. Sariya Bin Zunaim, a companion of the Prophet, was then on a military expedition in Persia. When he returned, he said that he had heard a voice crying out, 'The mountain, O Sariya, the mountain!' That sound propelled him to go to the top of the mountain near which he happened to be, and thereby gain victory. This famous legend is about telepathy (takhāṭur), and seems to have occurred to the author by association with the mountain that was confiscated to build the Israeli settlement. I read this as an ironic comparison between past victory and present helplessness.

Page 54 | 'Today, part of it, or all, may show . . . what might show'—This verse is attributed to Duba'ah Bint Amir, the subject of a number of legends. It is said that she was beautiful, and therefore highly desirable, and that she had hair that was long enough to cover her body. However, even hair that long was bound to move out of place in the process of circumambulation, and what her verse is saying amounts to this: 'Parts or all of my femininity may show, but that does not make me available.' The words she uses are *lā uḥilluh*—literally, 'I do not make it licit.'

Of all the Arabic websites that allude or discuss this legend, the most sensible version is the one found at www.dorar.net/hadith/sharh/17700

Page 57 | 'the Inner Monastery is a blessed olive tree'—For the author, the Inner Monastery, a Christian monument, is a complex and universal symbol that is tied up with his historical identity as a Palestinian, his existential identity as a writer and person as well as his cultural identity as a Muslim. It is not a dead ruin but a living olive tree, like the other olive trees in the orchards. The words about the 'blessed olive tree' are drawn from the one of the most beautiful verses in the Qur'an: 'God is the light of the heaven and the earth. / His light is like a niche in which is a lantern, / The lantern in a glass, / The glass like a shimmering star, / Kindled from a blessed tree, / An olive, neither of the East nor of the West, / Its oil almost aglow, though untouched by fire, / Light upon light!' (24 [*al-Nūr*]: 35).

Page 58 | 'In the rubble is our rose . . . slowly'—These are the first four lines of Darwish's poem, 'Poems About an Old Love', which first appeared in 1966 in *A Lover from Palestine. Collected Poems* (Beirut: Dar al-Awda, 1996, VOL. 1, p 130).

Page 59 | 'I called him "Áthar"'—This name [ism, also 'noun'] is an action [fi'l, 'action', also 'verb'.] Yes, an action—for action is important in life. It comes from the same root that gives us āthār ['ruins, traces'] and īthār ['altruism']. I called him 'Áthar' but I did not realize that with this name I was going to return to my āthār- ['ruins', 'traces'] and to what I have 'preferred' [āthar-tu].' With the double meanings of ism and fi'l, the first sentence could also have been translated, 'This noun is a verb.' There is a kind of intersection in language here where the name and the verb are crossing paths with the action and the noun. Language is talking to itself, extending the range of its semantic possibilities.

Looking at the Arabic words included in the quotation, we note that they all emanate from the basic root 'athar' (short, unstressed first vowel) that connects the name Áthar (pronounced 'āthar', with a long and stressed first vowel), with ruins (āthār, with both vowels long) in general and Barghouthi's ruins in particular. Barghouthi's ruins could be a reference to the Inner Monastery from where the voice came, or to the state of a body ravaged by cancer. Since āthār also means traces, a return to them could also signify the traces of his walks in the orchards, or the traces he will leave behind in the landscape after his death. There is a hint of a reference here to writing as well, since—in addition to meaning 'ruins'—āthār is also used to refer to the writing an author leaves behind after his death. In the final analysis, these writing will be the only meaningful historical traces Barghouthi will leave behind. This complex word play on the name of his son highlights the community of meaning waiting to be discovered under its umbrella. Language reaches into his son's name as the olive reaches into the oil. It is all part of the same process. The colour purple is associated with the Phoenicians.

Page 66 | 'the last ghreriya in these mountains'—The Arabic word for 'goyim' is aghyār, which sounds suspiciously close to what an irregular plural of ghrerī might sound like if it existed.

CHAPTER TWO: LAND OF TALES

Page 69 | 'blue flowers of the basalon shrub'—I have not been able to find the scientific name of this shrub. The word başalon is related to başal ('onions'), but from his description of it as a shrub and from the colour of its flower, it does not appear to be an onion. There is mention of a başalon as a type of onion (başal al-başalon) at: hoptolov.ru/ar/okna-i-otkosy/vyrashchivanie-luka-batuna-uhod-za-posevami-uborka-urozhaya-luk-batun.html, but (as far as I can determine) this plant does not belong the onion family.

Page 74 | 'That which already passed . . . has already passed'—This line is frequently attributed to al-Mutanabbi but is not found in his dīwan ('collected poems'). I am indebted to Muhammad Siddiq for alerting me to this fact.

Page 75 | 'How cramped life would be, except for the space that hope provides'—This is a well-known line from a poem called 'Lāmiyyat al-'Ajam' by a writer of the Abbasid Period who is known as al-Tughrā'ī. It is thought to have been composed around 1111 AD. There is a very good translation of this poem by J. N.

Mattock: Al-Tughrā'ī, 'Lāmiyyat al-'Ajam', *Journal of Arabic Literature* 13 (1982): 53–7. The quoted line is the second part of a thought about hope that was started in the line before it (lines 39–40). Here is Mattock's version of both lines: 'I beguile my soul with hopes and keep watch for them / How straitened life would be, but for the wide plain of hope' (p. 56).

Page 76 | 'It's as if I had died . . . I know this vision'—'It's as if I had died before now' is a citation from 'Mural', Darwish's long poem about his own near-death experience:

> It's as if I had died before now . . .
> I know this vision, and know that I
> am heading to an unknown . . .
> —*Jidarīya* ('Mural'), p. 11., Joudah, p. 102

'Regardless how astray far into it the needles may go'—*mahmā am'anat fī ghayyihā al-ibaru*. The key word here, astray (*ghayy*), occurs a number of times in the Qur'an, most famously in the verse about religious tolerance (*lā ikrāha fī al-dīn*): 'There is no compulsion in religion / Right guidance has been distinguished from error (*ghayy*)' in Khalidi's translation, though 'from error' may—equally cogently—be rendered, 'going astray' (2 [al-Baqarah]: 256). My translation of *ghayy* as 'going astray' rests on its polarity with *rushd* ('right guidance') as set down in this verse.

'Should the tips of your hair . . . O stones of the house, pray!'—Cited from Darwish's poem 'To One Who Is Lost' from the 1967 volume, *Ākhir al-Layl* ('The Last Part of Night'), *Collected Works*, VOL. 1, p. 224. My translation.

'miserable evening during the Khamsin winds'—The Khamsin is an 'oppressive hot, dry, and dusty south or southeast wind' occurring in North Africa and the Eastern Mediterranean . . . in late winter or early summer'. It is thought to blow for fifty (*khamsīn*) days. Accessible online under 'Khamsin wind'.

Page 77 | 'a moment of Sufi Illumination'—In the Sufi and later philosophical traditions in Islam, ishrāq (or 'illumination') refers to the apprehension of truth through a light emanating from God (Hikmat al-Ishrāq, 'wisdom by illumination'), described in Qur'an (24:35) as 'the Light of the heavens and the earth'.

Page 78 | 'is it the storm in which . . . the country itself dissolves'—Citation from the Egyptian poet, Muhammad Afifi Matar.

Page 79 | 'like the ecstasies of the Sufis'—The expression shaṭḥāt ṣūfiya (literally, 'Sufi trips') designates the unorthodox spiritual and ecstatic experience of Sufi trances. It is the phrase used for these experiences in Sufi discourse, and in writings about the Sufis. The orthodox approach sees faith (religion) as a happy balance between 'reason' (the human mind) and 'revelation' (the Qur'an). To emphasize the supernatural quality of the light, the author compares it to the shaṭḥāt ṣūfiya—the ecstasies that cannot be explained in terms of conventional religious categories. See Carl W. Ernst, *Words of Ecstasy in Sufism* (1985), for a thorough discussion of the Sufi ecstasies.

'And our strange story—the wind ripped it apart'—Quotation from Feiruz's song, You're Not My Sweetheart' ('Lā Inta Ḥabībī').

Page 80 | 'I imagined I was a butterfly in pomegranate blossoms'—Citation from Darwish's poem, 'Don't Sleep . . . My Love', from the 1967 volume, *Ākhir al-Layl* ('The Last Part of Night'). *Collected Works*, VOL. 1, p. 181.

'If I were to laugh . . . the rain would fall'—The Motif of Magic Rain (D902) is encountered in Palestinian folktales especially with reference to unusual heroines, for example, in 'Little Nightingale the Crier'. See *Speak, Bird, Speak Again*, p. 103. Here Barghouthi places himself in the middle of a folktale in the guise of a heroine, switching gender as his son wanted to do earlier in the text.

Page 82 | 'I escape to the house, and sit for hours . . . or sleeping'—I think we can assume that sitting 'for hours, even days, without movement, gazing at a point in front of me on the floor' is a description of deep meditation. Later in the text he says that he 'saw the olive tree from the perspective of . . . timeless time.'

Page 83 | 'the man from the Daʿwa movement . . . People of the Cave'—Sirwāl is Palestinian Arabic (mentioned again later) for which there is no proper English equivalent. It is a loose-fitting gown that covers the body. It is casual, and to be distinguished from the qumbāz, a more formal and lined garment (with pockets). The sirwāl can be tied around the middle and worn under the aba, or cloak, or, in more recent times, under a Western-style jacket.

Daʿwa means 'call'. The Call movement claims to be 'God's way of bringing believers to the faith . . . Militant sub-movements interpret daʿwa as calling Muslims back to the purer form of religion practiced [the Prophet] Muhammad and the early Muslim community'. Accessible online under 'Dawah'.

The 'People of the Cave': A reference to the legend of the seven sleepers who hid inside a cave outside Ephesus to escape Roman persecution some time around 250 CE, and emerged three hundred years later. Their story is told in Surah 18 (The Cave) of the Qurʾan. Judging from his appearance, wearing the sirwāl, the sandals and the beard, the Daʿwa person appears to belong to another era, like the sleepers in the cave.

Page 84 | 'The orange illuminates . . . the jasmine is innocent'—Cited from Darwish's poem about Palestine, 'Qatalūki fi al-Wādī' ('They Killed You in the Valley'), from the 1972 volume, *Uḥibbuki Aw Lā Uḥibbuki* ('I Love You, Or I Love You Not'). *Collected Works*, VOL. 1, p. 423.

Page 85 | 'The first time they brought me . . . so far away from me'— Cited from the poem, 'Today Is Sunday,' by the famous Turkish poet Nazim Hikmet. My translation is from the author's Arabic version. I do not know if Barghouthi had read it in Arabic or English translation. For a different version, see www.poemhunter. com/poem/today-is-sunday/ Yet another version may be found here: www.marxists.org/subject/art/literature/ nazim/sunday.html

Page 88 | 'Who, after you, lives a kingship . . . of his dreams'—Aghmat is a town in Morocco, 30 km to the southeast of Marrakesh. It is where Al-Mu'tamid died in prison in 1095 CE, and where his grave is located. He is a highly regarded poet, especially the lament for his earlier life that Barghouthi cites, from which both lines are taken.

Page 89 | 'Where are you from? . . . the country of windows'—Both 'where are you from' citations are from a song by Feiruz, called 'S'hirna, S'hirna' ('We Stayed Awake').

Page 90 | 'Every night I sing . . . and start walking'—From the 'Farewell' song ('I now must say goodbye'—'Anā ṣār lāzim waddiʿkun') by Feiruz. Because Barghouthi is using this song as a musical emblem of his own departure, I have decided to provide the full text in translation:

> I must now say goodbye, and will say something
>   about me
> My simple story is that, if not for you, I wouldn't be
>   singing
> We sang songs written on papers
> We sang the songs of someone full of longing
> But in the end, the time will come to say good-bye
> O people, I must tell you this story about myself
> I feel everything I'm saying as it comes pouring out
> My musicians have played and parted
> And the audience too is slowly parting
> And always, in the end, the time will come to say
>   good-bye

Tomorrow I'll be back with you
If not tomorrow, then the day after for sure
You must keep talking to me, and I will hear you
Even if the voice were faint and came from far away
Without our music, the night would be sad
It would be a night without a song
Every night I sing in a different city
Then pick up my voice and start walking

CHAPTER THREE: WHEN THE FOXES DO NOT ARRIVE

Page 91 | 'The night and I were walking ... seeing you'—From a song by Feiruz called '*Sahrit Ḥubb*' ('An Evening of Love').

Page 92 | 'Your uncle's life is hard!'—The word 'uncle' here does not indicate kinship. It is an honorific title, used to address, or refer to, an older male—in this case to the poet himself.

'I am not one of those who guard ... on top of scorpions'—This line is from Al-Mutanabbi's poem whose first line begins 'Bring back my morning' which also serves as the title of the poem.

Page 94 | 'By which window did I stand? ... And when was it that there was not?'—'Wa matā kān mā kān'—literally, 'And when was it that there was not?' It is clear from the text so far, with its ghoulah's lanterns, the tales his mother tells him and the strange goings on in the 'no-place' (like the mountain, the moonlit orchards, the wadis and the line of the horizon), and the movement back and forth in time that the author is drawing on the world of folk and fairy tales to create an atmosphere of the marvellous. The question he asks here (matā kān mā kān?) confirms our suspicion because the expression kān mā kān ('there was, there was not') is the most frequently used opening for a folk or fairy tale—to confirm that the events taking place in the no-time and the no-place are fictional. The expression has a double meaning that hinges on the fact that mā is both a relative pronoun ('that' or 'what'), and a negative particle ('not'), thus yielding 'there was (kān) what (mā) there was (kān),' as well as 'there was' (kān) and 'there was not' (mā kān). Therefore, the author's question, matā kān mā kān ('when was, what there was not') cannot be translated, or answered for that matter, because in effect he is asking, 'when (matā) is the imaginary real?' In other words, 'Where am I? In fact, or fiction?'

Page 95 | 'less than a ghost'—The clause kān mā kān discussed in the previous note is based on configurations of the verb kāna ('to be'). That is also the case for the text about the fox: adraka ('it [the fox] realized') annanī ('that I am') ghayru qādirin ('not able') ʿalā al-hujūmi ʿalā ('to attack') ayyi ('any') kāʾinin (noun from kāna, 'a being'), kāʾinan (verbal noun from kāna, 'myself being' [since I am]) min (from) aw mā kān ('or there was not') . . . so he passed by me kaʾannanī ('as if I were . . .'). The word kaʾannanī is related to the verb kāna not in meaning but in its alphabetic shape, consisting of the same three letters k-a-n, as kānā). We note also the harmonies based on the sound of the letters /k/ and /n/ that unite annanī, kāʾinin, kāʾinan, kaʾannanī and mā kān. We further take note of the extensive use of kaʾanna ('as if') throughout the text, the intention being (as noted above) to place the entire action of the memoir in the fairy tale state of 'as if'.

'The course of rivers that seek . . . deliverance from diaspora'—These lines are from Darwish's 1990 poem, 'The Tragedy of Narcissus, the Comedy of Silver' ('*Maʾsāt al-Narjis, Malhāt al-Fiḍḍa*' about Palestinian exile and a tragically imagined (non)-return. In the original the lines are as follows:

> They are, as they are, the very nature of all rivers that
> seek no permanence
> Roaming the world, hoping the way may lead to the
> path of delivery from diaspora
> —*Collelcted Works*, VOL. 2, p. 422.

'I am as I am, one of those who are as they are . . .'—Barghouthi here seamlessly merges Darwish's 1990 experience of exile ('roaming the world' being the condition of Palestinian diaspora par excellence) into his own. He does this by making Darwish's first sentence part of his own text, with the subject personalized. 'They are as they are' (kānū kamā kānū) becomes 'I am as I am.' He then repeats the thought by using Darwish's exact words but without commas and quotation marks, as part of his own lead-up to the quotation ('I am as I am, one of those who are as they are.') We note again his fascination with the verb kāna ('to be'), as in the previous Note, and that may have been why he chose to cite this particular passage from Darwish in the first place.

Page 96 | 'via "the path of deliverance from diaspora" . . . its outcome in a certain experience'—The meaning here is not clear due to the author's Barghouthi's reliance on the discourse of philosophy, and possibly Sufism, without offering clarification: darb al-najāt min al-shatāt al-ladhī badā darban naḥwa *al-maḥdūd* fī al-tajriba wa *al-mutanāhī* fīhā. The emphasized words are technical terms in Islamic ontology, where *al-mutanāhī* (that which has the nature of coming to an end, that is, the finite) is contrasted with *al-lā-mutanāhī*, the infinite. In Sufism, *al-maḥūd fī al-tajriba* and *al-mutanāhī* both belong to the same sphere, that of ordinary human experience.

The word shatāt also has religious connotations, implying a wandering mind, or absence of concentration in prayer or meditation. The Darwish poem that Barghouthi quotes is definitely about Palestinian exile, but given that this memoir is suffused with desire for spiritual experience, he may be taking advantage of double meanings to refer to his yearning to transcend the existential exile of ordinary experience—a state of permanent *shatāt*. Earlier, he refers to the Mountain as 'the ladder of spirit'. On this understanding, then, the infinite in this memoir is indicated by the 'line of the horizon' where the finite meets the infinite. In the sentence immediately following the text quoted above, he uses the word *ascent*, and mentions the first heaven of the Pharaohs, having just referred to himself again as a shadow. The Mountain here thus becomes a symbol for spiritual experience.

Page 98 | *'Enuma Elish'*—The Babylonian creation myth.

Page 99 | 'The Arabs used the word baṭara . . . which eventually became ṭarab'—The presumed derivation of *ṭarab* from *Petra* most likely belongs to the genre of folk etymology. The import of using language to create a non-existent relationship is to connect the unconnected—to put language at the centre of experience. We saw earlier Barghouthi's reflection on the relationship of cities to the names of people, where he suggested that people with the same name are residents of the city of their name, and are connected by virtue of that fact.

'soft rain in a distant autumn'—The title (and first line) of the poem by Darwish, 'Soft Rain in a Distant Autumn':

> Soft rain in a distant autumn
> The birds are blue
> And the land is a festival
> —from his 1969 volume, *The Birds Are Dying in Galilee* (al-*Aṣāfiru Tamūtu fi al-Jalīl*). *Collected Works*, VOL. 1, p. 254.

Page 99–100 | 'The dagger / enters the heart . . . No.'—Translation by Ralph Angel. See aprweb.org/poems/poem-of-the-solea-trans-lated-by-ralph-angel5

Page 100 | 'Write with blood . . . blood is spirit'—These words are from *Thus Spoke Zarathustra*: 'Of all that is written, I love only what a person has written with his blood. Write with blood, and you will experience that blood is spirit.'—*The Portable Nietzsche*, p. 152.

'the music of Ziad al-rahbani'—Ziad al-Rahbani is the son of Feiruz, the Lady of Lebanese song, and a famous (Arabic) jazz musician in his own right.

Page 101 | 'Among his names are "the Genius" . . .'—Baudelaire: 'Genius is no more than childhood captured at will, childhood equipped now with man's physical means to express itself, and with the analytical mind that enables it to bring order into the sum of experience, involuntarily amassed.' See www.goodreads.com/quotes/120604-genius-is-no-more-than-childhood-recaptured-at-will-childhood

Page 103 | 'of the film *Red Desert*'—*Red Desert* (1964) is a film by the Italian director, Michelangelo Antonioni.

Page 104 | 'O tree of time . . . tree at a crossroads'—From the song, 'Sharjat al-ayyam' ('The Tree of Days').

Page 105 | 'Satih who used to fold his body'—The story of Saṭīḥ occurs in *Biḥār al-Anwār* (*Seas of Light*), for which, see en.wikipedia.org/wiki/Bihar_al-Anwar. For Saṭīḥ, see en.wikipedia.org/wiki/Rabia_ibn_Nasr

'I, Tiresias, saw all of this'—This is a summary citation from *The Wasteland* rather than a direct quotation. Eliot's line is, 'I, Tiresias, old man with wrinkled dugs / Perceived the scene, and foretold the rest.' See https://www.poetryfoundation.org/poems/47311/the-waste-land, Part III, 'The Fire Sermon.'

Page 106 | '"Alone," Shakespeare said . . .'—I have not been able to find a direct source for this quotation that would fit Barghouthi's sense of isolation better than Hamlet's soliloquy in Act II, Scene (ii), Line 519–20, where he says, 'Now I am alone. O, what a rogue and / peasant slave am I!'

Page 107 | 'Deemed solitude fellowship . . . stars finds hers'—Imru' al-Qays was one of the greatest poets in Arabic literature. A pre-Islamic poet, his influence on the course of Arabic poetry has been incalculable. For information on the Zanj Rebellion, see en.wikipedia.org/wiki/Zanj_Rebellion

A difficult line in which the poet praises a cousin of his named Shums Ibn Malek. The 'mother of intertwined stars' is the Milky Way. There is an Arabic proverb about the stars as guides. I was guided in my translation primarily by *Al-Mukhassas* of Ibn Sīdah, VOL. 6, p. 250. Another helpful resource is available online (in Arabic):almerja.net/reading. php?i=6&ida=575&id=556&idm=19727

Both resources may be accessed online by searching the first half of the line—*yarā al-waḥdata al-unsa al-anīsa*—in Arabic script.

'Listen to the crowd . . . in their ears!'—The lines from *The Death of Cleopatra* are discontinuous quotations from the opening scene of the play.

Page 108 | 'The wolf howled . . . I almost flew away'—The line is by the Abbasid poet Al-Uḥaymar Al-Saʿdī, famous for being an antisocial brigand. See https://poetsgate.com/poem.php?pm=92600

'Beauty will not save the world . . . in this world'— This frequently quoted line is adapted from Dostoevsky's *The Idiot*: 'Is it true, Prince,' asks Hippolyte Terentiev of Prince Myshkin, 'that you once said, "It is beauty that will save the world?"' See a-heedful-idiot.blogspot.com/2012/05/beauty-will-save-world.html

Page 113 | 'I would write "Gypsy song"'—The 'Gypsy Song' is a collaboration with the Palestinian musical group Sabreen, accessible online, with English translation, at 'sabreen gypsy song'.

'the first one weeps . . . made of garnets'—This is the first poem in the volume, *Poem of the Deep Song* (1987, p. 2):

The river Guadalquivir
winds through orange and olive trees.

The two rivers of Granada
descend from the snow to the wheat

Ay, love
That went away and never returned!

The river Guadaquivir
has whiskers of garnet.
The two rivers of Granada,
one weeping and the other blood.

Ay, love
that went away through the air!

The name of the river that runs through the heart of Seville, Guadalquivir, is a Spanish combination of two Arabic words, wadi (frequent occurrence in this memoir) and kabir (large, grand).

'Ancient / land of oil lamps . . . and arrows'—Translation by Ralph Angel. This is the first poem in the series *Poem of the Solea*. The solea is one of four poetic genres that Lorca explored in *Poem of the Deep Song*. See aprweb.org/poems/poem-of-the-solea-translated-by-ralph-angel5

Page 114 | 'I'll come to you . . . you a carnation'—These lines occur in the third stanza of 'Victim No. 18,' from the 1967 volume, *The Last Part of Night*, p. 211.

Page 115 | 'the Two-Horned Alexander'—Alexander the Great, referred to in Arabic as the 'Two-Horned', is a mysterious figure who appears in the Qur'an (18: 83–98), where he is called Dhū al-Qarnayn (the 'two-horned one'). His appellation is itself the subject of much speculation. He is the subject of many legends, like the one the author tells, and the hero of many romances, similar to those of Al-Zir Salem that Qaddura sings in this memoir but which havez now disappeared from Palestinian oral tradition.

Page 115–16 | 'In Macedonia, he sent a dream . . . fell upon the ground'—Barghouthi added the following note at the end of this paragraph: 'See E. Wallis Budge, *Egyptian Magic*, pp. 95–8.' Rather than retranslate Barghouthi's translation, I have chosen to quote directly the segment from *Egyptian Magic* that corresponds to Barghouthi's summary of it. Accessible online at 'Budge Egyptian Magic pdf', p. 224.

Page 119 | 'I see what I want of the ladder'—This is the first line of the fifth quatrain of poem titled 'Rubāʿiyyāt ('quatrains'), which is the sequence of poems that opens the 1970 collection ʿArā Mā Urīd' ('I See What I Want') by Darwish. *Collected Works*, VOL. 2, p. 379. Here is the whole quatrain:

> I see what I want of the ladder. I do see
> A gazelle, and grass, and a stream . . . and close my
>   eyes
> The gazelle is sleeping in my arms
> And its hunter sleeps, near his children, in a distant
>   place.